I0811417

STRENGTHENING INTEGRITY AND ACCOUNTABILITY IN CHURCH LEADERSHIP

CHRISTIAN OKON EKONG

CONCORDIA PUBLISHING HOUSE · SAINT LOUIS

This study is dedicated to my beloved wife, Offiong, for her continuous faithful partnership in both ministry and all of my life.

Concordia Publishing House

Founded in 1869 as the publishing arm of The Lutheran Church—Missouri Synod, Concordia Publishing House gives all glory to God for the blessing of 150 years of opportunities to provide resources that are faithful to the Holy Scriptures and the Lutheran Confessions.

Copyright © 2019 Concordia Publishing House
3558 S. Jefferson Ave., St. Louis, MO 63118-3968
1-800-325-3040 • cph.org

All rights reserved. No part of this publication may be reproduced, stored in a retrieval system, or transmitted, in any form or by any means, electronic, mechanical, photocopying, recording, or otherwise, without the prior written permission of Concordia Publishing House.

Scripture quotations are from the ESV® Bible (The Holy Bible, English Standard Version®), copyright © 2001 by Crossway, a publishing ministry of Good News Publishers. Used by permission. All rights reserved.

Quotations from the Small Catechism by Martin Luther are taken from *Luther's Small Catechism with Explanation*, copyright © 1986 Concordia Publishing House. All rights reserved.

Manufactured in the United States of America

2 3 4 5 6 7 8 9 10 28 27 26 25

CONTENTS

FOREWORD

THE Lutheran Leadership Development Program (LLDP) is proud to present *Strengthening Integrity and Accountability in Church Leadership* as the second volume of the program's resource. Earlier this year Concordia Publishing House (CPH) published *Breath of God, Yet Work of Man: Scripture, Philosophy, Dialogue, and Conflict*. Coauthored by Dr. Albert B. Collver III and the Rev. Charles P. Schaum, the book was used by Dr. Collver himself when he taught for the LLDP the World Lutheranism and Ecumenical Movement course in February. The present volume will serve as a resource for the Ecclesial and Organizational Leadership course. The author, the archbishop of Lutheran Church of Nigeria, the Rev. Dr. Christian O. Ekong, will be the instructor this November. Our plan is to produce a book for each course of the LLDP. These volumes will then be properties of CPH as the premier publishing house of world Lutheranism.

It was the wisdom of the International Lutheran Council (ILC) to launch the LLDP as a certificate program in response to the need of the Lutheran church bodies around the world that are seeking leadership development for current and future leaders in the areas of Lutheran identity and basic business administration. On January 5, 2017, the representatives of ILC, CPH, Concordia Theological Seminary in Fort Wayne, Indiana (CTSFW), and The Lutheran Church—Missouri Synod (LCMS) signed the protocol document to plan this program. Soon after, this writer was appointed as the program director.

The program runs by way of forming cohorts of eight to twelve men who take twelve courses in two years. The first cohort participants happen to all come from the African continent—from Ethiopia, Tanzania, Madagascar, South Africa, Ghana, and Nigeria. Their responses to the first four classes are overwhelmingly positive. They said: "These courses have been eye-openers for me. The scales fell from my eyes." "I think these courses must be shared among churches to awaken and keep the leadership informed." "I wish I had taken these courses many years ago." "This arrangement of courses and the program is commendable. It is my wish that the ILC is able to provide continuous opportunity for potential church leaders of churches in Africa and other parts of the continent." "To be confessional Lutheran is not so easy in my part of Africa. This program has given me an opportunity to get connected with other confessional leaders in Africa." "This program has given me exactly what I needed and fellow pastors of my church need. Thank you so much!" In addition to such words on the program in general, the participants have expressed their deep appreciation for each course. So far, the following four courses have been completed: Theology of the Lutheran Confessions, World Lutheranism and Ecumenical Movement, History of the Lutheran Church, and Lutheran Hermeneutics.

Strengthening Integrity and Accountability in Church Leadership is a welcomed resource for church leadership. Originally, it was prepared as a Doctor of Ministry project dissertation, which Archbishop Ekong successfully defended in May 2018. Now that it is being printed in this way, the results of his meritorious research have an opportunity to be spread and read—in the United States, throughout the African continent, and in other countries. The strength of this volume is that it was written by a faithful and proven church leader. An equally important value of this book is that it was written by a Nigerian archbishop. Our prayer is that *Strengthening Integrity and Accountability in Church Leadership* may provide for an international readership wisdom and experience of leadership in the church. The LLDP is deeply grateful for the partnership of CPH. May the Lord continue to richly bless the worldwide churches that confess Jesus and all He has taught, which is faithfully repeated in the Book of Concord.

Rev. Naomichi Masaki, PhD
Director of LLDP
Professor of Systematic Theology
Concordia Theological Seminary
Fort Wayne, Indiana, USA

A WORD OF ENDORSEMENT

As a bishop in the Evangelical Lutheran Church in Tanzania (ELCT), I was very happy to read *Strengthening Integrity and Accountability in Church Leadership* by Archbishop Christian Ekong of the Lutheran Church of Nigeria. First, this is a very important book for churches in the African context. Second, it is very nice to see a book for the African context, written by an African churchman. All too often, leadership books are written from a Western perspective containing advice that is not always helpful from a Global South perspective.

Dr. Ekong argues that it is necessary to strengthen both integrity and accountability among church leaders, particularly in the Lutheran Church, if the leaders want people to follow them. Ekong states that many church leaders lack integrity and accountability, instead loving the position and the benefits the position brings—such as power, money, and social standing—more than they love the people they serve and the church.

Ekong identifies the many challenges the churches in Africa face, such as poverty, laziness, incompetence, misuse of funds, enmity, tribalism, corruption, disease, and witchcraft. Some church leaders approach these challenges with dishonesty and nonaccountability, resulting in a misuse of power which erodes the trust people have in their leaders and the church. Sometimes church leaders get others to collude with them, resulting in embezzlement, theft, fraud, extortion, favoritism, and nepotism.

Ekong states that a church leader should follow the way of Christ and His apostles, leading with gentleness, kindness, integrity, honor, and patience. A faithful leader lives under the shadow of the cross, facing many hardships. Yet Jesus has promised to bless those who are persecuted and suffer for His sake.

I believe this book will be helpful both in the African context and for churches around the world. This work identifies some of the problems church leaders face, offers some solutions, and provides a way to analyze and examine how church leaders can be Christlike, having integrity and honor in the face of many difficult problems.

I hope the study is read and can assist Lutheran Churches in Africa and around the world.

Dr. Emmanuel Makala, Bishop
South East of Lake Victoria Diocese, Shinyanga
Evangelical Lutheran Church in Tanzania
http://elct-selvd.org

INTRODUCTION

As I write this on the Martyrdom of John the Baptist, the appointed psalm comes to mind. "In you, O Lord, do I take refuge; let me never be put to shame!" (Ps. 71:1). This is the prayer Dr. Ekong would have all church leaders pray as they face the many challenges and difficulties of being a church leader today. The church leader faces many temptations which might cause him to lose integrity and be put to shame. For the church leader who seeks to lead with integrity and accountability, those forces who want to take advantage of the church and squander its resources for personal gain will lead under the shadow of the cross. The faithful church leader will suffer a martyrdom of sorts, if not physically often emotionally and spiritually. Yet Ekong notes that a leader is to be like Jesus and His apostles, who shepherded God's people and protected them from the wolves. It is not an easy task or one for the faint of heart. Ultimately, a leader will only have followers if he leads with integrity and accountability.

Dr. Ekong began this study as his dissertation for the Doctorate of the Ministry program at Concordia Theological Seminary in Fort Wayne, Indiana, after personally witnessing the challenges leaders face in Africa. He also has witnessed corrupt leaders in the church. With the dominance of prosperity gospel theology, which shares some similarities to ancestor worship among non-Christians, Ekong desires to demonstrate that seeking a leadership position for personal gain does not actually create followers. People follow leaders, especially church leaders, who have integrity and are accountable with the resources they have been given to manage.

This work focused on the leaders in the Lutheran Church of Nigeria, yet it has broader application both to churches in Africa and around the world. The first half of the book examines some of the theoretical and philosophical underpinnings behind leadership in the church. The second half of the book provides an example on how a church leader could conduct a study himself, providing a methodology, surveys, and sample letters. The second half of the book uses the Lutheran Church of Nigeria as an example.

This book is being published as the second in the series for the Lutheran Leadership Development Program (LLDP) sponsored by the International Lutheran Council (ILC). LLDP was conceived to help Lutheran church leaders gain skills both in theology and practical matters. Dr. Ekong's work is valuable in this effort, especially since he writes from the perspective of an African church leader who has experienced the items he discusses as he served as both the archbishop of the Lutheran Church of Nigeria and as the chairman of the Africa region for the ILC.

Rev. Albert B. Collver, PhD
On the Martyrdom of John the Baptist 2019
Manchester, MO

PREFACE

ON Monday, February 18, 2019, the International Lutheran Council (ILC) commenced the Lutheran Leadership Development Program (LLDP) in collaboration with Concordia Theological Seminary, Fort Wayne, Indiana. The program, though not degree awarding, is intended to build the capacity of emerging confessional Lutheran leaders through formal theological education sessions both theoretically and practically. Here is where experiences of practicing faithful and confessional Lutheran leaders will show the promise of sharing. The majority of the participants in the Development Program would come from the global south—Africa, Asia, and South America.

I shall never forget the compliment of my academic dean, Professor Charles Gieschen, who said to me, "You are such a great blessing to the Doctoral Program and indeed the Post-Graduate School of Concordia Theological Seminary, Fort Wayne, because of your vast leadership experience in ministry which according to your professors is reflected in your enriching contributions during classes. We are in deep appreciation of you."

Although my project may seem to present very Western leadership principles, I have reflected a lot on practical African experiences in my leadership of the Lutheran Church of Nigeria, the Lutheran Communion in Central and West Africa, the International Lutheran Council, and the Christian Council of Nigeria. I have proposed that church leadership which wishes to be adjudged as possessing strength through integrity and accountability in human relations must be based upon Christ's justification of the leader through faith.

It is very important for every reader of this project to reflect on the relationship between Karl Marx's theory of materialism, Max Weber's theory of idealism, and Peter L. Berger's theory of dialecticism. On the whole, the Marxist theory of materialism has played out in today's prosperity gospel or theology of glory which dominates the African continent. Thus we are confronted with the need to be more encouraged and persuaded by the theology of the cross. Only the theology of the cross strengthens integrity and accountability in the leadership of Church, be it the Lutheran Church of Nigeria or elsewhere.

Christian Ekong
President/Archbishop
Lutheran Church of Nigeria

ACKNOWLEDGMENTS

I am indeed very thankful to my wife for encouraging me to undertake doctoral study in ministry in order to make a contribution to the Church at the end of the program.

My project adviser, the Reverend Professor Robert Roethemeyer is a great servant of God, who is very tolerant and always ready to guide me toward success. He made my task of working on this project very easy. He clarifies my thoughts, making me see my proposal through to become a reality.

Members of my project committee, the Reverend Professors Timothy Quill and John Nordling, relate to me not so much as professors but as friends, brothers, and colleagues. Their encouragement is unimaginable.

All the professors who have lectured in all the courses that I have taken leading to the award of this Doctor of Ministry (DMin) degree are highly appreciated. They demonstrated exemplary dedication to ensuring that both the on-campus and off-campus studies were worthwhile. I will always remember the CTSFW faculty for offering me the opportunity to undertake higher theological education at this level (the highest professional degree in Lutheran ministry).

Professor Lawrence Rast, the president of CTSFW, and Professor Charles Gieschen, the academic dean, routinely asked me how I was doing and made sure everything was going well with me in my studies and ministry.

Professor Naomichi Masaki, though he did not teach me directly during this project, made sure that he encouraged my adviser to treat my case with dispatch.

The many assistants to different directorates, International Studies, Graduate School, DMin Program, etc., were always available and ready to help. Mrs. Cindy Johnson with Mrs. Judith Bascom were there for me at all times.

The Rev. Robert Smith has shown me typing skills that I will treasure forever. He showed me how to work with various settings on the computer, which I personally would not be interested. He took time to assist in arranging this work in an acceptable manner.

Uduak Mike, my secretary, would not be left out of this acknowledgment list. She was burdened the most, owing to my limited ICT skills and time. Many times I rewrote that which she does not find clear enough.

My respondents and the leaders of the Lutheran Church of Nigeria are greatly appreciated for the support in prompt and candid opinions during the period of my experiments which led to the completion of this project.

The LCMS President, the Rev. Dr. Matthew C. Harrison; the Director of Church Relations, the Rev. Dr. Albert B. Collver; the Director of International Studies, the Rev. Dr. Timothy Quill are the hands from which this special blessing of advanced theological education comes to me. Thank you is not enough to express how much joy it is in my heart to be sponsored through this program.

My church, the Lutheran Church of Nigeria, deserves my thanks for giving me cover by which I undertook this study.

All persons, most especially my wife and children whose time with me as husband, friend, and father respectively was limited, deserve my heartfelt gratitude.

Again, thank you for your great support morally and otherwise! In all, I give God the glory.

CHAPTER ONE

INTRODUCTION

1.1 Background of the Study

Two of the fundamental traits or qualities of church leadership are integrity and accountability. Lack of these traits brings about discouragement in followers.[1] Anytime there is human leadership, there are opportunities to exhibit a substantial level of integrity and accountability. People can only lead those who have developed trust in them. To live with integrity and accountability means that your private life matches the values you promote in your public life.[2]

Christians are called to place the needs of others ahead of their own, to be the servant of all. Yet Christians are in a constant battle to meet these expectations and to live lives of integrity and accountability. From Scripture to the modern news media, we have story after story exposing the painful fact that the private lives of church leaders do not always match the messages presented from the pulpit. When this happens, the leaders have failed to demonstrate accountability and integrity.

Accountability requires church leaders to exhibit transparency and demonstrate that they are faithful with the financial, material, and immaterial property of the church. In terms of administrative functions, some church leaders hide their salaries, the ways the ministry spends money, and how much money is donated to the ministry. This creates doubt in the integrity of the administrative process of the church. Instead, Christian churches should be willing to open their financial records and should always follow

[1] Louis W. Fry, "Toward a Theory of Spiritual Leadership," *The Leadership Quarterly* 14, no. 6 (December 1, 2003): 693, accessed February 18, 2019, http://www.sciencedirect.com/science/article/pii/S1048984303000547.

[2] Raed Awamleh and William L. Gardner, "Perceptions of Leader Charisma and Effectiveness: The Effects of Vision Content, Delivery, and Organizational Performance," *The Leadership Quarterly* 10, no. 3 (September 1, 1999): 345, http://www.sciencedirect.com/science/article/pii/S1048984399000223.

best practices for financial record keeping. Church leaders exhibit integrity and accountability when they seek to learn from Christian groups the best ways to be good financial and spiritual stewards of God's assets.

Trust is at the heart of leadership and is based on the integrity demonstrated by the leader. If trust is destroyed, there will be no one to lead, which is why leadership—even in the church—is earned by demonstrating trustworthiness and not betraying those who follow. Integrity is important in church leadership because: it protects church leaders (Ps. 25:21), and it gives leaders confidence (Prov. 10:9). Integrity enhances a leader's ability to make better decisions (Prov. 11:3). It reflects well on the Lord (1 Chron. 29:17). Integrity sets leaders apart and allows them to create a bond of trust with their followers.

Integrity has taken a beating. We live in a world in which self-interest seems to triumph over character and integrity. Pastors and church leaders are not immune to the temptation to spin, to cut corners, or to compromise. Yet Christ, whom we serve, lived a life of integrity, and He expects leaders to do the same by His power.[3]

Accountability in leadership means leaders act consistently with their commitments and are responsible for their actions or decisions, including responses to circumstances.[4] Leaders are accountable when they own all of their actions. Frequently, when desired outcomes or results do not materialize, people make excuses to explain why they did not happen. Those who can explain honestly why a result was not produced are as accountable as those who actually produced the result. When leaders are able to lay out the actions they took and the actions they did not take for a given outcome, they are accepting accountability.

Frequently, leaders encounter circumstances and situations beyond their control. Leaders who demonstrate accountability identify adequate and appropriate responses in such difficult situations. What you did or did not do to respond effectively demonstrates whether you fulfilled your commitment. Over time, being accountable allows leaders to build power and to sustain strong performance when they have been effective and to identify the root cause of breakdown when they are not effective.[5] Lord Acton said

---

[3] Dag Heward-Mills, *The Art of Leadership*, 2nd ed. ([Accra, Ghana]: Parchment House, 2006), 11.

[4] Deanne N. Den Hartog et al., "Culture Specific and Cross-Culturally Generalizable Implicit Leadership Theories: Are Attributes of Charismatic/Transformational Leadership Universally Endorsed?" *The Leadership Quarterly* 10, no. 2 (June 1, 1999): 219.

[5] Radostina K. Purvanova, Joyce E. Bono, and Jessica Dzieweczynski, "Transformational Leadership, Job Characteristics, and Organizational Citizenship Performance," *Human Performance* 19, no. 1 (January 2006): 11.

that "power tends to corrupt and absolute power corrupts absolutely."[6] There are many temptations for the leader. It is not easy handling success or failure.

Not every person can handle a top leadership position. Leadership in any circumstance changes a person—sometimes for the better; sometimes for the worse. Leaders who put in extra effort and work can gain more position, more power, and more privilege. However, each one of these benefits can create a platform for temptation that can be a source for the downfall of a leader if care is not taken to handle it well. A leader is at risk of enjoying his position more than serving his neighbors or constituents. The Scriptures call such leaders "belly servers" (Phil. 3:19) as they seek after position, power, and privilege. Thus, as church leaders, God has not left us without caution: "Therefore let anyone who thinks that he stands take heed lest he fall" (1 Cor. 10:12).

Although leaders often have special gifts, it is the marriage of these gifts with the needs of a particular group of people or organization that brings the greatest opportunities for success. This explains the dynamism of the individual who exhibits accountability in church administration. This leader is presumed to possess strong shepherding skills and democratic, visionary, and motivational leadership styles, among others.[7]

Leadership in churches may accept a high level of responsibility and accountability in order to achieve its primary objective, which is the growth of the Gospel. Doing so inspires a spirit of cooperation from the subordinates, and they become encouraged based on the principles and ethical processes used in managing social interactions and relationships.

Church leadership to some extent is based on a divine calling[8] to serve in the vineyard of the almighty God. One may be chosen by God to serve as a teacher, evangelist, pastor, apostle, or prophet. These are leadership positions, and portfolios are meant for those who are endowed with these leadership positions in the church throughout the world. This divine calling makes church leadership different from appointments in professional settings such as medicine, education, and governance, among many others. Thus this study seeks to strengthen the integrity and accountability of those in church leadership positions, particularly leaders in the Lutheran Church. While this study has applicability in the West, its primary focus is on church leadership in Africa.

---

[6] Elizabeth Knowles, *The Oxford Dictionary of Quotations*, 5th ed. (Oxford: Oxford University Press, 1999), 1, entry 16.

[7] Bill Hybels, *Courageous Leadership* (Grand Rapids: Zondervan, 2002), 12.

[8] John E. Akpami, *Vision: Equipping Church Workers for Effective Leadership* (Kaduna, Nigeria: TW Press & Publishers, 2002), 110.

1.2 Statement of the Problem

In today's world, people with accountability and integrity are hard to come by. It is quite disheartening when church leaders no longer show integrity and accountability. Church leaders fail in their responsibilities to others in the church because most of them are not conscious of the fact that they can be tempted to misuse power. The shepherding of the church is in the hands of overseers, pastors, elders, etc. But this is not an excuse to abuse the influence granted to them by exploiting people and misusing the power. Promotion from one position to another in the church is not given in order to make leaders into little dictators.

Leaders may be fine Christians until they get a promotion. Once promoted, they may start teaching the people in demeaning, derogatory ways, and sometimes they make excessive demands on the people, as well as show some levels of dishonesty and a lack of accountability. Also, church leaders may fail to discharge their responsibilities acceptably. Besides ignorance, they can be tempted to abuse their power. Furthermore, church leaders are exposed to the temptation of profiting from their privilege of leadership, which gives the people reasons to question their motives.

The role of pastors and other church leaders is not to hold down the people but to serve their needs and to equip and elevate them to serve Jesus and change the world. When church leaders understand that the power God gives to them is not for themselves but for others, then the virtues of integrity and accountability will be strengthened.

A number of studies have been carried out by scholars to seek a way of curbing or reducing lack of integrity and accountability. This study is conducted to help fill the existing gap by way of strengthening integrity and accountability of leadership in the Lutheran Church, particularly African Lutheran churches.

1.3 Specific Objectives

The objective of the study is to look for ways to strengthen integrity and accountability of leaders in the Lutheran Church. The specific objectives are:

1. To examine the level of integrity and accountability of those in leadership positions in the Lutheran Church.
2. To discover any elements of dishonesty and nonaccountability found among those in leadership positions in the Lutheran Church.
3. To find out the possible factors which bring about dishonesty and nonaccountability among those in leadership positions in the Lutheran Church.

4. To determine the intent behind and the purpose of strengthening integrity and accountability of those in leadership positions in the Lutheran Church.
5. To find out the barriers to the effective strengthening of integrity and accountability of those in leadership positions in the Lutheran Church.
6. To determine the strategies that can help strengthen the integrity and accountability of those in leadership positions in the Lutheran Church. To make useful recommendations for theological exercise of those in leadership positions in the Lutheran Church.

1.4 Research Questions

The following questions will be answered (in particular with examples from those in leadership positions in Lutheran Church of Nigeria):

1. What is the level of integrity and accountability of those in leadership positions in a Lutheran church?
2. What are the different elements of dishonesty and nonaccountability found in some leaders in a Lutheran church?
3. What are the possible factors that bring about dishonesty and nonaccountability among leaders in a Lutheran church?
4. What is the intent behind and the purpose of strengthening integrity and accountability of those in leadership positions in a Lutheran church?
5. What are the barriers to the effective strengthening of integrity and accountability of those in leadership positions in a Lutheran church?
6. What are the strategies that can help strengthen the integrity and accountability of Lutheran church leaders?

1.5 Hypotheses

The following hypotheses will be tested:

1. There is no significant relationship between the integrity of the leaders in a Lutheran church and the members' perception of their leadership effectiveness.
2. There is no significant relationship between the accountability of the leaders in a Lutheran church and the members' perception of their leadership effectiveness.

3. There is no significant relationship between the integrity of the leaders in a Lutheran church and the members' "followership."
4. There is no significant relationship between the accountability of the leaders in a Lutheran church and the members' "followership."
5. There is no significant influence of the integrity of the leaders in a Lutheran church and people's membership in the church.
6. There is no significant influence of the accountability of the leaders in a Lutheran church and people's membership in the church.
7. There is no significant influence of age on the level of integrity of the leaders in a Lutheran church.
8. There is no significant influence of age on the accountability of the leaders in a Lutheran church.
9. There is no significant difference in the level of integrity and accountability of the leaders in a Lutheran church before and after teaching concerning integrity and accountability.

1.6 Significance of the Study

This work is beneficial to those who want to serve Christ truthfully and who seek the true meaning and correct application of biblical texts. This work is relevant to the everyday experience of human life in a fallen world, and it works toward providing a correct biblical and theological perspective concerning the issues of dishonesty and nonaccountability of church leaders.

This work is also important in particular to African society as church leaders work to decrease the tension created by the high level of dishonesty, nonaccountability, and lack of integrity among church workers. The attributes of honesty, accountability, and integrity directly affect church growth and development. This theologically balanced study will explore how these traits affect the "followership" and membership of Christians in Lutheran churches, particularly those in Africa. This work will provide a framework for further and refined discussions concerning church leadership and the ways to strengthen integrity and accountability.

1.7 Delimitation of the Study

This study was based on research conducted among members of Lutheran Church of Nigeria (i.e., members of LCN Board of Directors, members of LCN zonal boards, members of LCN district boards, LCN church councillors, LCN seminary faculty members, LCN Schools Management board members, Lutheran high school principals, past presidents of LCN, past vice presidents of LCN and past district chairmen-lay, other workers of the church, and lay members of congregations throughout South-South geo-political zones in Nigeria). Through the questionnaire and seven key interviews, the study records members' perception of the integrity and accountability of leaders in Lutheran Church of Nigeria and the effects of these traits or the lack of them on the "followership" of members, the possible factors that can lead to dishonesty and nonaccountability, and the ways that integrity and accountability can be strengthened among church leaders.

CHAPTER TWO

LITERATURE REVIEW

2.1 Theoretical Framework

2.1.1 Marx's Theory of Class Conflict

Leadership in Africa has been greatly affected by the prosperity gospel, which is the false doctrine that God rewards with physical blessing, in a kind of automatic way, any request from people who have proven themselves to be faithful Christians. Phrases like "name it and claim it" are common in this type of teaching. The analysis of the prosperity gospel involves the study of several sociological factors, such as social class, religion, and economy. It can be further explored by examining religion from two different schools of thought: Karl Marx, who treated religion as an dependent variable, and Max Weber, who treated religion as an independent variable. To summarize these two views, Marx thought economics influenced religion while Weber thought religion influenced economics. Marx was a materialist while Weber was an idealist. Much of this section is based upon Bradley A. Koch's dissertation "The Prosperity Gospel and Economic Prosperity: Race, Class, Giving, and Voting."[1]

According to Koch, the prosperity gospel seemingly explains why some people are poor while others are wealthy. It provides a means for the poor to move themselves upward while at the same time providing justification for the wealthy who hold an elevated status. Leaders who can appeal to the poor by offering hope and who can appeal to the rich by justifying their status can obtain followers, not to mention personal power and wealth.

Socioeconomic class may determine the flavor of religion a person chooses. This might seem to favor Marx's view that religion is a dependent variable rather than Weber's view that religion is an independent variable (that is, not dependent on a person's socioeconomic status).

[1] Bradley A. Koch, "The Prosperity Gospel and Economic Prosperity: Race, Class, Giving, and Voting," (PhD dissertation, Indiana University, 2009), 11–14.

For this reason, it is helpful to review briefly Koch's analysis about these two schools of thought. Marx rooted his theory of class conflict in materialism. Marx believed that material existence, such as a person's socioeconomic status, was an independent variable and predicted other dependent variables such as religion. Although Marx did not fully develop a theory of religion, he did make some well-known comments, including:

> Religious suffering is at one and the same time an expression of real suffering and a protest against real suffering. Religion is the sigh of the oppressed creature, the sentiment of a heartless world, and the soul of soulless conditions. It is the opium of the people.[2]

Marx argues that religion results from the economic condition in which people find themselves. H. Richard Niebuhr, reflecting on the rise of denominationalism, divisions, and schisms in the Church, noted that denominationalism can be explained by examining religious history with an economic interpretation.[3] Although Niebuhr did not discount theological differences in the denominations, he thought economics influenced the formation of a religious community or denominational affiliation more than theology. Or perhaps the economic conditions of a people group influenced the development of the theology.[4]

In contrast to Marx, Weber was an idealist. He believed that ideas superseded materialism and could shape the material world, rather than the material situation shaping the ideas. (This, of course, is an oversimplification but does help to express the main differences in approach.) Weber notes how an idea causes the world to change perspectives much like a train changing tracks. Weber writes: "Very frequently the 'world images' that have been created by 'ideas' have, like switch men, determined the tracks along which action has been pushed by the dynamic of interest."[5]

Although Weber recognizes that religion can be influenced by a person's economic situation, he primarily focuses on how religion influences a person's material situation, including his economic situation. Weber would argue that Protestantism, particularly Calvinism, led to the development of modern capitalism. Calvinism teaches the doctrine of predestination. This

---

[2] Karl Marx, *Early Writings*, ed. Quintin Hoare, trans. Rodney Livingstone and Gregor Benton (New York: Penguin Books, 1975), 224.

[3] H. Richard Niebuhr, *The Social Sources of Denominationalism* (Hamden, Conn.: Shoe String Press, 1954), 26.

[4] Sabine Boerner and Christian Freiherr von Streit, "Transformational Leadership and Group Climate Empirical Results from Symphony Orchestras," *Journal of Leadership & Organizational Studies* 12, no. 2 (July 21, 2016): 57, accessed February 19, 2019, https://journals.sagepub.com/doi/pdf/10.1177/107179190501200203.

[5] Max Weber, *The Protestant Ethic and the Spirit of Capitalism* (New York: Scribner, 1930), http://archive.org/details/protestantethics00webe.

means that before the foundation of the world, the Lord determined who would be saved and who would be damned. Lutheranism and some other groups hold that the Lord determined who would be saved but not who would be damned. Calvinism is unique among Christian confessions in teaching that the Lord also determined who would be damned. Calvinism seeks for signs that a person might be predestined for salvation. One such sign that a person will be saved is the accumulation of wealth as the blessing of God upon a person's righteous life. The accumulation of wealth frequently is connected with hard work. Hard work and wealth fits nicely with the idea of capitalism. Weber thought that religion helped create the upper classes and perhaps helped explain why the lower classes existed. Thus, in contrast to Marx, Weber thought religion influenced the material situation more than the material situation influenced religion.

New studies exist that support Weber's thesis over that of Marx. Koch notes that sociologist Gerhard Lenski conducted a survey of Detroit-area residents in 1958. He asked if religion affected people's secular lives. The overwhelming response he received found that religion affected people's economic and political views, as well as their views about education and science. Thus he concluded that Marx was wrong and Weber was correct.

Naturally, academics often seek a middle course between two diametrically opposed views. Koch notes that in 1990, Peter Berger attempted to find a middle ground between Marx and Weber. Instead of choosing either Marx's view or Weber's view, he looked for a both/and relationship. Berger concludes that a person's material situation influences his ideas (religion) and that a person's ideas (religion) influence his material situation.

People who study religion and sociology have tried to place the prosperity gospel within the dialectic between Marx and Weber. This allows for the study of the prosperity gospel not only as a theological phenomena but also as a sociological one. Unmentioned by any of these frameworks is the distinctly African one, in which traditional religion and ancestor worship fit into some of the dynamics of the prosperity gospel.

In this particular case study, the economic situation of Christians in Uyo, Nigeria, can help predict their level of attention and reception to the prosperity gospel. This, in turn, influences how they understand faith's effect on prosperity, human development, socioeconomic status, etc. In some ways, the prosperity gospel is the connection between religion and Marx's economic and social theories.

The prosperity gospel offers hope to the poor while at the same time provides justification to the rich for their status. Yet, as Lutherans, who are biblical Christians, the theology of the cross offers salvation and eternal life on the basis of "justification by faith alone." Jesus said, "If anyone would come after Me, let him deny himself, and take up his cross daily and follow Me" (Luke 9:23). No man can save himself, whether poor or rich. We cannot save ourselves; that is why Jesus encourages us to deny ourselves. Jesus urges the Christian to acknowledge that it profits a man nothing if he gains the whole world and forfeits his soul. The cross that we take up with Jesus daily is our sin and the result of sin in this world. Jesus welcomes us to Himself, saying, "Come to Me, all who labor and are heavy laden, and I will give you rest. Take My yoke upon you, and learn from Me, for I am gentle and lowly in heart, and you will find rest for your souls. For My yoke is easy, and My burden is light" (Matt. 11:28–30).

Martin Luther teaches that a man is justified not because of what he can do when he says, "I cannot by my own reason or strength believe in Jesus Christ, my Lord, or come to Him; but the Holy Spirit has called me by the Gospel . . ."[6]

When considering the appeal of the prosperity gospel to the poor as offering hope for upward mobility and to the rich as providing justification for their status, it is important to remember that Jesus Christ justifies us through faith, for eternal salvation. Jesus teaches that "man shall not live on bread alone, but on every word that comes from the mouth of God" (Matt. 4:4).

2.1.2 Goals Theory of Organizational Effectiveness by Hoy and Miskel (1982)[7]

The goals theory of organizational effectiveness is based on the conceptualization of organizational effectiveness in terms of goal attainment.[8] In this regard, the day-to-day activities of an effective organization meet or exceed its goals. The three common types of organizational goals include official goals, operative goals, and operational goals.[9]

Official goals are formal statements of purpose made by the governing board of the organization, such as the board of directors or board of governors. The official goals portray the mission of the organization. Operative goals, on the other hand, reflect the true intention of the organization. They mirror the actual tasks or activities performed by the organization. Official

---

[6] Martin Luther, *Luther's Small Catechism with Explanation* (St. Louis: Concordia, 1986), 26.

[7] Wayne K. Hoy and Cecil G. Miskel, *Educational Administration: Theory, Research, and Practice* (New York: Random House, 1982).

[8] Robert J. House, "Path-Goal Theory of Leadership: Lessons, Legacy, and a Reformulated Theory," *The Leadership Quarterly* 7, no. 3 (September 1, 1996): 265, accessed February 19, 2019, http://www.sciencedirect.com/science/article/pii/S1048984396900247.

[9] Graeme Currie and Andy Lockett, "A Critique of Transformational Leadership: Moral, Professional and Contingent Dimensions of Leadership within Public Services Organizations," *Human Relations* 60, no. 2 (2007): 341–70.

goals are general while operative goals are specific. Operative goals are used by the administration to direct staff behavior. Operative goals carry with them approved criteria and evaluation procedures that indicate how the levels of accomplishment will be measured.

The goals theory of organizational effectiveness assumes that a rational group of decision-makers in the organization has rational goals to be pursued and that the goals are few enough to be measured and are concretely defined enough to be understood by the participants. It heavily relies on particular administrative practices to enhance goal specifications and goal achievement. Such administrative practices include management by objectives (MBO), cost/benefit analysis, and behavioral objectives.

The goals theory of organizational effectiveness was studied by Hoy and Miskel in the educational environment. The school system is an organization which establishes rational, specific, and general goals which must be attained.[10] For example, students' excellent academic performance in the final school certificate examinations, students' ability to gain admission into higher institutions, students' performances in the sciences, and students' performance in sports are some of the operational goals which principals should strive to achieve. The theory reminds principals of the need to adopt relevant administrative practices to enhance the attainment of the established goals. Principals are expected to define and specify the established goals and to work toward their attainment by facilitating the availability of resources in their schools.

2.1.3 Systems Resources Theory of Organizational Effectiveness by Yuchtman and Seashore (1967)[11]

Systems resources theory of organizational effectiveness defines successful organizations as those that use a position of strength within its environment to gather necessary resources.[12] The bargaining is continuous and becomes an ingrained process in the organization as it competes with other groups for funds, equipment, and even personnel. In the long run, some organizations are able to achieve their goals while others are not. Thus the criterion for effectiveness in this theory is the organizational ability to secure resources.

[10] David M. Boje and Carl Rhodes, "The Virtual Leader Construct: The Mass Mediatization and Simulation of Transformational Leadership," *Leadership* (August 11, 2016): 407, accessed February 19, 2019, https://journals.sagepub.com/doi/pdf/10.1177/1742715005057232.

[11] Ephraim Yuchtman and Stanley E. Seashore, "A System Resource Approach to Organizational Effectiveness," *American Sociological Review* 32, no. 6 (1967): 891–903.

[12] House, "Path-Goal Theory of Leadership," 287.

The assumption with systems resources theory of organizational effectiveness is that an organization is an open system that exploits its environment. In this regard, effective organizations are those that are able to develop new behaviors and techniques that could lead to the acquisition of more valued resources. A major generalization of this theory is that in more effective organizations, bureaucratic expectations, informal groups, and individual needs work together more harmoniously to influence the environment than they do in less effective organizations.

One study of systems resources theory of organizational effectiveness explored the institutional challenges to teachers' instructional effectiveness. The study found that principals needed to work with the teachers for the provision and maintenance of resources in their schools. Principals and teachers who worked harmoniously were able to acquire more valued and scarce resources. Thus achievement of the rational goals of an organization heavily rely on administrative practices. The administrative goals guide staff behavior.[13] The results of this study can be applied to a Lutheran church as a system that has goals: pastors and bishops are to teach the Word of God. For the Lutheran Church effectively to attain its goals, it needs to secure scarce and valued resources—both human and nonhuman.

2.2 Conceptual/Empirical Review

2.2.1 Integrity and Accountability in Church Leaders

Leadership is a conceptual phenomenon that lacks specific definition from researchers. Okoronta views leadership as the ability to give guidance to those who are willing to follow to complete the mission statement of an organization such as the church.[14] To give guidance, leaders must have a clear picture of the future outcome. Leadership also involves the capacity to work hard and to be enthusiastic about turning visions into reality and encouraging followers to do the same.

Bennis and Goldsmith have identified three necessary functions of leadership: first, leaders "are responsible for the effectiveness of the organization"; second, leaders "rally subordinates/constituents around a common purpose," creating a stable and confident organization; third, leaders "project a confidence in integrity."[15] Leadership is a complex phenomenon which

---

[13] Currie and Lockett, "A Critique of Transformational Leadership: Moral, Professional and Contingent Dimensions of Leadership within Public Services Organizations," 341.

[14] G. O. Okoronta, "The Impact of Leadership Styles in the Pentecostal Churches on the Growth of the Gospel in Kaduna State" (Ahmadu Bello University, 2015), 16.

[15] Warren G. Bennis and Joan Goldsmith, *Learning to Lead: A Workbook on Becoming a Leader*, 4th ed., rev. and updated (New York: Basic Books, 2010), 11, http://public.eblib.com/choice/publicfullrecord.aspx?p=515497.

combines the personal traits of an individual and the dominant variables in an organization.[16] Leadership is getting a group of people to see things from the leader's point of view. It is a great responsibility in which those who have taken it up pay with their lives.[17] It is a process of influencing others to act and to accomplish a specific goal.[18] Leadership is guiding, instructing, directing, or compelling subordinates to follow or to obey instructions and directions.[19]

According to Myles Monroe, leadership is "the capacity to influence, inspire, rally, direct, encourage, motivate, induce, move, mobilize, and activate others to pursue a common goal or purpose while maintaining commitment, momentum, confidence, and courage."[20] According to Jan Francois Lourens, leadership "is one of the most complex and multifaceted phenomena to which organizational and psychological research has been applied." It is like beauty, which is hard to explain.[21] Thus it is an ability to get people to achieve a result, knowing that leadership is not a title or position; rather, it consists of performance. [22]

Leadership remains a fundamental process in every organization, and it is the means by which an organization builds a style of orderly operation.[23] In the church specifically, leadership involves a series of vital roles such as teaching, counseling, discipline, and policy implementation, and coordination, recruitment, and retirement of staff for the growth of the organization.[24] The characteristics or personality traits embedded in an individual church leader to some extent must include elements of accountability. Hence the church leader who is not accountable to followers may have the disposition to dishonesty that would destroy the integrity of the leader.

---

[16] Nwakibiye P. C. Nwolise, *Traditional Administration in Nigeria: Historical Perspective, Theory and Practice* (Port Harcourt, Nigeria: Paragraphics, 2009), 12.

[17] Heward-Mills, *The Art of Leadership*.

[18] Dale S. Beach, *Personnel: The Management of People at Work*, 5th ed. (New York: Macmillan, 1985), 121.

[19] R. C. Onuogu, *Creative Leadership* (Lagos, Nigeria: Touchlife, 2008), 13.

[20] Myles Munroe, *The Spirit of Leadership: Cultivating the Attributes That Influence Human Action* (New Kensington, Penn.: Whitaker House, 2005), section 5.

[21] Jan Francois Lourens, "Change-Centred Leadership and Various Correlates" (PhD dissertation, University of Pretoria, 2007), 199, http://hdl.handle.net/2263/24931.

[22] John E. Akpami, *Leadership with Results* (Kaduna, Nigeria: TW Press & Publishers, 2006), 11.

[23] Okoronta, "The Impact of Leadership Styles in the Pentecostal Churches on the Growth of the Gospel in Kaduna State," 15.

[24] Okoronta, "The Impact of Leadership Styles in the Pentecostal Churches on the Growth of the Gospel in Kaduna State," 16.

Some authors classify leadership in the world into categories of political leadership, economic leadership, and sociocultural leadership, among others. Although these categories in practice operate in the church, yet church leaders should not make these leadership classifications sacrosanct, knowing that they are in the vineyard of God. That is to say, church leaders should be aware of the environment, the people involved in the setting, knowing that each of the leadership types operate based on the principles required within the settings.

To a great extent, church leadership survives due to the accountability level of the leader. A church leader who conceals financial activities, physical properties, and other economic activities of the church is capable of mismanaging the church properties. Such a church leader would not support that account reconciliation meetings be held and would always create confusion among committee members or those who are concerned with the financial health of the church.

Christ instituted the Church (as seen in 1 Cor. 12:28). It is the whole body of the faithful, whether in heaven or on earth, who have been spiritually united with Christ as their Savior. The Church provides a regular mind-changing forum for anyone and helps the way one thinks, reasons, and behaves.[25]

The church is a place where lives are transformed, and this means that the church leadership has a great responsibility to their congregations. Because of the unique attributes of a church as an organization, its leaders, though similar to leadership in other organizations, have unique tasks for which unique abilities and gifts are needed.[26] The single greatest contributor to the effectiveness of and the ability of a church to grow is its leadership.[27] Yet the church is pictured in the New Testament as a unique organism, more than an organization. Each group of individual believers is to work together and is part of the Body of Christ.[28]

The basic difference between a business and a church is that each church member is vital to the healthy functioning of the whole. Thus church leaders focus on the health of the church and all its members, not being content merely to check off every item on their to-do list. Good organization is

---

[25] Heward-Mills, *The Art of Leadership*, 11.

[26] Peter L. Berger, *The Desecularization of the World: Resurgent Religion and World Politics* (Washington DC: Ethics and Public Policy Center, 2008), 131.

[27] Norman Shawchuck and Roger Heuser, *Leading the Congregation: Caring for Yourself While Serving Others* (Nashville: Abingdon Press, 1993), 11.

[28] Wayne Cordeiro, *Doing Church as a Team: The Miracle of Teamwork and How It Transforms Churches* (Ventura, Calif.: Regal Books, 2005), 12.

required, but not at the expense of maintaining the big picture.[29] According to George Barna, a church leader "is called by God to lead; leads with and through Christlike character; and demonstrates the functional competencies that permit effective leadership to take place."[30] The Christlike character is then seen as the ability of a leader to urge other people to cooperate to such an extent that they do tasks with trust and enthusiasm. These characteristics exhibited consistently are indicators of integrity, which the church leaders should possess.

A church leader's integrity may have an influence on their effectiveness in leading in the church. Integrity has a positive effect on leaders and church organizational effectiveness. History and practiced experience continue to demonstrate the highest levels of integrity are required to prevent dishonesty.[31]

Leaders who are guided by personal integrity and values are more likely to act according to the organization's values and to act morally, with consistency, and with the best interests of others in view.[32] Although actions that seem to lack integrity—not taking responsibility for failure or taking credit for the successes of others—can bring success,[33] "principle-centered leadership [is] the foundation of all leadership activities."[34] For example, Tony L. Simons defines the concept of Behavioral Integrity as "the perceived degree of congruence between the values expressed by words and those expressed through action."[35] But this measurement only looks at the level to which actions match stated intentions—not the "morality" of either.

2.2.2 Elements of Dishonesty and Nonaccountability in Church Leadership

Leaders in whatever capacity often escape accountability even in the church. Because of pretense, high levels of dishonest behaviors are often hidden. Those who lack accountability make excuses, shift the blame,

---

[29] Berger, *The Desecularization of the World*, 131.

[30] George Barna, *Leaders on Leadership* (Ventura, Calif.: Regal, 1997), 21.

[31] Thomas E. Becker, "Integrity in Organizations: Beyond Honesty and Conscientiousness," *Academy of Management Review* 23, no. 1 (January 1, 1998): 160, accessed February 22, 2019, https://journals.aom.org/doi/10.5465/amr.1998.192969.

[32] Joseph L. Badaracco and Richard R. Ellsworth, *Leadership and the Quest for Integrity* (Boston: Harvard Business School Press, 1989), 3.

[33] Robert Jackall, *Moral Mazes: The World of Corporate Managers* (Oxford: Oxford University Press, 2010), 122.

[34] Stephen R. Covey, *Principle-Centered Leadership* (New York: Summit Books, 1991), 15.

[35] Tony L. Simons, "Behavioral Integrity as a Critical Ingredient for Transformational Leadership," *Journal of Organizational Change Management* 12 (1999): 90.

exhibit poor work habits, and pretend not to know how to do aspects of their job. They complain but don't work. And such lack of accountability can quickly spread through an organization.[36] Leaders know the reasons behind actions and avoid rationalizing their decisions, especially when outcomes are less than ideal.

Some church leaders are seriously dishonest and embrace corruption. They become dishonest to themselves and support a corrupt society, sometimes employing corrupt scriptural interpretations. They perpetrate an attitude of monetizing the Word of God, to the extent that they convert prayers into money, property, and other valuables for personal benefit. Most of them divert church resources or funds to their own bank account. They defraud followers by the use of misleading scriptural interpretation to induce them to donate money or property.[37]

Notably, church leaders can extend their dishonesty to extortion in terms of coercive incentives from followers. Thus they use dangerous scriptural messages and expose members to false spiritual teachings in order to attract donations and gifts. Besides, most of them are dishonest to themselves in order to abuse their discretion.[38] They create bureaucratic structures in the church and claim oversight or accountability structures, yet siphon all the monies. By doing so, they neutralize the bureaucratic effectiveness of their structures so that they can implement embezzlement behaviors.

In addition, some church leaders in their leadership styles exhibit favoritism, nepotism, and clientelism. They pretend to act in the interest of the church and followers, not displaying self-interest openly, but subtly putting forward a particular group, family member, or ethnic group as most capable for a job.[39] These practices occur often in the hiring and promoting of staff—thus showing lack of integrity in the leadership of the church. Yet these behaviors are mainly for self-aggrandizement.

---

[36] Thomas H. Bivins, "Responsibility and Accountability," in *Ethics in Public Relations* (Thousand Oaks, Calif: Sage Publications, 2006), 31.

[37] Organization for Economic Co-operation and Development, *Integrity in Public Procurement: Good Practice from A to Z* (Paris: OECD, 2007), 11.

[38] David Banisar, *Freedom of Information around the World 2006: A Global Survey of Access to Government Records Laws* (London: Privacy International, 2006), 13.

[39] Organization for Economic Co-operation and Development, *Integrity in Public Procurement*, 13.

2.2.3 Dishonesty Factors and Nonaccountability in Church Leadership

Nonaccountability refers to the deliberate refusal to establish a checks-and-balances system to protect an organization or group of individuals from harm to themselves and to others. It is the responsibility of leaders to perform, conduct, and ascertain procedures that would be ideal for that purpose.[40] Christian accountability checks on what leaders are doing, recognizing that leaders are responsible not only to their neighbor but also to God (Matt. 12:36; Rom. 2:16; 14:2; 1 Cor. 3:10–15, among others). It is noted that when a leader or group of leaders decline to employ a process of accountability, they are not acknowledging best practices.

Church leaders, who remain non-accountable, do not hold one another into account and are unable to fully develop important relationships with their family, friends, and co-workers, as well as volunteers and others in the church who belong to Christ's family. It makes them most arrogant whenever issues of the financial position of the church are raised and account reconciliations are reviewed. Nonaccountability tends to retard our heartfelt Christian journey to an atmosphere of trust. This is because it is infused with elements of dishonesty, lies, and other corrupt practices, as well as the inability to explain what they do, sometimes coupled with some incorrigible acts.[41]

According to Machiavelli, a leader is supposed to be "a man of compassion, a man of good faith, a man of integrity, a kind and religious man."[42] Without integrity, a leader becomes useless in these fundamental characteristics. This is because integrity is a concept that denotes the rational way of doing things that effect other people. It displays sincerity, honesty, and the respect of ethics and values.[43] Thus a church leader who is not accountable will not likely obey the principles, ethics, and values of their ministry. Such a leader would always increase ambiguity in financial activities, exhibit no

---

[40] Louis W. Fry, Steve Vitucci, and Marie Cedillo, "Spiritual Leadership and Army Transformation: Theory, Measurement, and Establishing a Baseline," *The Leadership Quarterly* 16, no. 5, Toward a Paradigm of Spiritual Leadership (October 1, 2005): 835, accessed February 22, 2019, http://www.sciencedirect.com/science/article/pii/S1048984305000779.

[41] Fry, Vitucci, and Cedillo, "Spiritual Leadership and Army Transformation," 835.

[42] Machiavelli, *The Prince* (New York: Penguin Books, 1983), 101.

[43] Vanessa Urch Druskat, "Gender and Leadership Style: Transformational and Transactional Leadership in the Roman Catholic Church," *The Leadership Quarterly* 5, no. 2 (1994): 99.

concern for others, and refuse to accept responsibility for the growth and nurturing of subordinates.[44]

Integrity (based off the Ten Commandments) includes the ability to:

- tell the truth
- obey the law
- reduce ambiguity
- show concern for others
- accept responsibility for the growth and nurturing of subordinates
- practice participation and not paternalism
- provide freedom from corrupting influences
- provide consistency across cases, and
- provide consistency between values and actions.[45]

Those who do not possess the highest levels of integrity cannot be church leaders.[46] The apostolic requirements in Holy Scripture make this abundantly clear (see 1 Timothy 3:1–7; Titus 1:6–9). Integrity in the service of the church is founded on the principles and behavioral standards which will serve as a resource for other church workers, both employees and volunteers. Church leaders who are not committed to justice and equity, not upholding the dignity of all people and their right to respect may not support accountability in their ministry. This caliber of church leaders will presumably oppress the poor and alienate or marginalize members by enforcing them to bring and contribute to the service of the Lord in order to fill their personal bank accounts.

The following factors of dishonesty exhibited by such leaders are widely thought to be as follows:

1. **Collusion.** This is the situation in which church leaders cooperate in an arrangement between two or more parties to achieve an improper purpose, including improperly influencing the actions of the church departmental head to collect money without the approval by the council. The most common form of collusion is when bidders agree among themselves on prices and "who

[44] J. G. Hunt, Kimberly B. Boal, and Ritch L. Sorenson, "Top Management Leadership: Inside the Black Box," *The Leadership Quarterly* 1, no. 1 (March 1, 1990): 41, accessed February 22, 2019, http://www.sciencedirect.com/science/article/pii/1048984390900149.

[45] Nemence Iriya and G. S. Namusonge, "Effects of Integrity on the Performance of Elected Leaders in Local Government Authorities In Maynard Region, Tanzania," *International Journal of Scientific & Technology Research* 4, no. 6 (June 2015): 84.

[46] Becker, "Integrity in Organizations," 160.

should win."[47] This includes leaders of the church, who influence the treasurer to deposit church finances into an account accessible to them. It may or may not involve paying bribes to the church officials so that they will turn a blind eye to the practice. Collusion also can involve determining the "winner" or "benefit" of a service or program in the church. In Africa, it may not be limited to a church leader's self or family, but also to his tribe or people group.

2. **Embezzlement and theft.** This is the taking or conversion of money, property, or other valuables of the church for personal benefit. It might involve diversion of ministry funds to the leader's personal bank account or taking the church property without the approval by the council.
3. **Fraud.** Fraud is the use of misleading information to induce someone to turn over money or property voluntarily, for example, by misrepresenting the number of people in need of a particular service. One way church leaders do this is to use the Word of God adversely to deceive someone to donate hugely in a voluntary manner for personal benefit. This is similar to a contractor using substandard materials in construction (with or without paying a bribe to the supervising engineer) for the purpose of making more money from a contract.[48]
4. **Extortion.** Extortion involves coercive incentives such as the use of threats of violence or the exposure of damaging information to induce cooperation.[49] Church leaders can be either the instigators or the victims of extortion. Extortion can also take the form of an official threatening to punish the official who refuses to certify or attest to misconduct of the leader.
5. **Abuse of discretion.** The abuse of an office for private gain, but without external inducement or extortion. Patterns of such abuses are usually associated with bureaucracies in which broad individual discretion is created or few oversights or accountability structures are present. Abuse of discretion can also be found in bureaucracies in which the decision-making of the religious

---

[47] R. Edward Freeman and Lisa Stewart, *Developing Ethical Leadership*, Bridge Papers (Charlottesville, Va.: Business Roundtable Institute for Corporate Ethics, 2000), 12.

[48] Freeman and Stewart, *Developing Ethical Leadership*.

[49] Robert S. Rubin, Erich C. Dierdorff, and Michael E. Brown, "Do Ethical Leaders Get Ahead? Exploring Ethical Leadership and Promotability," *Business Ethics Quarterly* 20, no. 2 (2010): 215.

norms is so complex as to neutralize the effectiveness of the accountability structures that do exist.

6. **Favoritism, nepotism, and clientelism.** In general, these involve abuse of discretion. However, in these specific cases, the act is governed not by the direct self-interest of the corrupt individual, but by some less tangible affiliation, such as advancing the interest of family (nepotism), a cabal, or ethnic, religious, or other groups. These practices occur often in the hiring and promoting of staff. However, they can also take the form of establishing a close relationship and giving assistance to the individual already in the leader's relations.

Church leadership concerns spiritual liberty and servitude. Thus "a Christian man is a perfectly free lord of all, subject to none. A Christian man is a perfectly dutiful servant of all, subject to all."[50] These are both statements of Paul: "For though I am free from all, I have made myself a servant to all, that I might win more of them" (1 Cor. 9:19); "Owe no one anything, except to love each other, for the one who loves another has fulfilled the law" (Rom. 13:8).

Even Christ, though Lord of all things, was made of a woman. He was made under the Law. He was at once free and a servant, at once in the form of God and in the form of a servant to redeem us all. This makes love by nature dutiful and obedient to the beloved.

Man is made up of both the old man and the new man. The spiritual nature is called the soul. This is the inward new man after Christ Jesus, redeemed through the washing of regeneration (Baptism). Paul writes: "We were buried therefore with Him by baptism into death, in order that, just as Christ was raised from the dead by the glory of the Father, we too might walk in newness of life" (Rom. 6:4).

This old man is sinful. The result of this diversity is that these two men oppose each other—the flesh lusts against the Spirit and the Spirit dislikes the flesh. "For the desires of the flesh are against the Spirit, and the desires of the Spirit are against the flesh, for these are opposed to each other, to keep you from doing the things you want to do" (Gal. 5:17).

It is important at this moment to discuss the means by which the inward man becomes free (justified) and a Christian—that is, a spiritual, new man. This happens absolutely without any outward thing. No outward thing has any influence in producing Christian righteousness or liberty (John 11:25; 8:36; Matt. 4:4). All the wants of the soul are provided for in and through the Word of God. Except by the Word of God the soul can do nothing because

---

[50] Martin Luther, "Treatise on Christian Liberty," trans. Henry Jacobs, in *Works of Martin Luther* (Philadelphia: A. J. Holman Company, 1915), 312. Also found in Martin Luther, *Three Treatises*, trans. Charles M. Jacobs et al. (Philadelphia: Fortress Press, 1970), 277.

its sufficiency is the Word—the Word is of life, of truth, of peace, of joy, of justification, of salvation, of liberty, of wisdom, of virtue, of grace, of glory, of love, and of every good thing (Psalm 119).

Reformation scholar John Witte describes Martin Luther's biblical anthropology as a paradox. He notes that Luther saw a person as both a sinner and a saint simultaneously, as well as a priest and a lord (master). Luther said that a human cannot do anything good but at the same time does nothing but good through faith. A human is totally free and yet is bound to his neighbor. The more a person recognizes himself as a sinner, the more holy the person becomes through faith. When a person is called to be a lord (master), he in fact becomes a greater servant to his neighbor. This is the paradox of human existence in faith. This dialectical theology is how Luther demolished the hierarchies that existed in the sixteenth century between the pope and princes, the clergy and the laity, the aristocrats and the commoners. Luther's teaching on the dignity of man was transformative in the realm of authority and liberty, and in the realm of church and state.[51]

The first care of every Christian leader ought to be to lay aside all reliance on works (Eph. 2:8–10) and strengthen his faith more and more, and by it grow in the knowledge not of works, but of Jesus Christ, who has suffered and risen again for him (1 Peter 5). Thus Christ, when the Jews asked Him what they should do to do the work of God, rejected the multitude of works that made them proud and demanded of them only one thing: "This is the work of God, that you believe in Him whom He has sent" (John 6:29).

Faith in Christ is an incomparable treasure, conveying salvation and preserving from all evil, as it is written: "Whoever believes and is baptized will be saved, but whoever does not believe will be condemned. And these signs will accompany those who believe: in My name they will cast out demons; they will speak in new tongues; they will pick up serpents with their hands; and if they drink any deadly poison, it will not hurt them; they will lay their hands on the sick, and they will recover" (Mark 16:16–18). Looking to this treasure, Isaiah predicted: "Though your people Israel be as the sand of the sea, only a remnant of them will return. Destruction is decreed, overflowing with righteousness. The Lord GOD of hosts will make a full end, as decreed, in the midst of all the earth" (Isa. 10:22–23). Is he not referring to faith as the complete fulfilling of the Law and offering those who believe such righteousness, that they will never be in need of anything else for justification? Paul writes: "For with the heart one believes and is justified, and with the mouth one confesses and is saved" (Rom. 10:10).

[51] John Witte, "The Freedom of a Christian: Martin Luther's Reformation of Law and Liberty," *Evangelische Theologie* 74, no. 2 (2014): 127.

In the same manner, the priesthood of Christ does not consist in the outward display of vestments and gestures as did the human priesthood of Aaron, but in spiritual things, in His invisible office:

- He intercedes for us with God in heaven;
- He performs all the duties of a priest;
- He teaches us inwardly in the Spirit with the living teachings of His Spirit.

Christ obtained two dignities at His birth and imparts and communicates them to every believer in Him. All believers in Christ are kings and priests in Him, as it is written: “You are a chosen race, a royal priesthood, a holy nation, a people for His own possession, that you may proclaim the excellencies of Him who called you out of darkness into His marvelous light” (1 Pet. 2:9). This is a spiritual power ruling in the midst of enemies and is powerful amid our distresses. It is strongly made perfect in weakness so that all things could be turned to profit us. Even the cross and death are compelled to serve us and work together for our salvation. This dignity is a true and almighty dominion, a spiritual empire in which all things work together for our good.

Faith works by love when a church leader applies himself with joy and love to the works of that freest servitude whereby he serves others voluntarily and not satisfying himself abundantly in the fullness and the wealth of his own faith. Teaching the Philippians that they had been made rich by that faith in Christ, Paul writes:

> So if there is any encouragement in Christ, any comfort from love, any participation in the Spirit, any affection and sympathy, complete my joy by being of the same mind, having the same love, being in full accord and of one mind. Do nothing from selfish ambition or conceit, but in humility count others more significant than yourselves. Let each of you look not only to his own interests, but also to the interests of others. (Phil 2:1–4)

The dignity and freedom of the Christian is a confession of Christ Himself: “For freedom Christ has set us free; stand firm therefore, and do not submit again to a yoke of slavery” (Gal. 5:1). What Christ did to win salvation in His divine and human natures, He now gives to those who by Baptism bear His name: Christian. God justifies the sinner by faith alone. The sinner is changed in the inner and outward man after the likeness of Christ. The Christian is free indeed in faith and a servant to all in works of love. Therefore, church leadership is a Christian life lived between these twin poles of faith and love. This is the paradoxical Christian freedom as Luther taught the church. This is also the dignity of every person in the church.

2.2.4 Intentions, Purpose of Integrity, and the Strength of Leadership Accountability

Every leader has intentions. These intentions may be positive or negative, good or bad, beneficial to either the leader, the organization itself, or to the members of the organization. Hence a successful Christian ministry is established on common values that are accepted by the constituency at large. When there is a diverse constituency with varied interests and desires, a strong leader will draw the group together by clearly articulating the common goals over and over again, especially by embodying these goals in his own life.

The leader inspires his employees and volunteers to increase their commitment to the organization and to embody the organization's values into their everyday lives. At this point, mostly, the intentions would be defined by whether the leadership has the genuine intentions for organization and the people that work toward organizational growth as well as achievement of its goals. This amounts to ethics of leadership and moral principles that guide individuals to adhere to the norms of accountability. Leadership in churches which goes along with high level of responsibility in order to achieve its primary objective—the growth of the Gospel—requires accountability. Through faithful preaching and teaching of the Word of God, the Holy Spirit, when and where He wills, gives growth. This leadership is capable of propelling a cooperative spirit of the members who would become encouraged based on the principles and ethical processes used in managing social interactions and relationships.

The leader helps create stakeholders, who believe that they share in the wins and successes of the organization, and also are responsible for short comings. If the leader of an organization has a great success, the stakeholders believe they achieved or helped achieve that goal also. If the organization fails to meet a goal, the stakeholders also feel as if they did not do all they could to help or could have done more to help the goal be achieved.[52] Setting goals and objectives in the church is a good practice, but it is only the Holy Spirit who gives growth, when and where He chooses, through faithful preaching of the Word and proper administration of the Sacraments.

For 2,000 years, the Church has emphasized serving. Servant leadership characterizes biblical leadership.[53] The focus on servant leadership in the Church was modeled after Jesus Christ, providing vision and purpose for Christian ministry. Jesus told us that He came to seek and to save the

---

[52] Akpami, *Vision: Equipping Church Workers for Effective Leadership*, 110.

[53] Michael Cooper, "The Transformational Leadership of the Apostle Paul: A Contextual and Biblical Leadership for Contemporary Ministry," *Christian Education Journal* (March 14, 2018): 48, https://journals.sagepub.com/doi/pdf/10.1177/073989130500200103.

lost and to be among us as a servant, so also faithful church leaders. Paul modeled the ministry of Jesus by giving of himself:

> But whatever gain I had, I counted as loss for the sake of Christ. Indeed, I count everything as loss because of the surpassing worth of knowing Christ Jesus my Lord. For His sake I have suffered the loss of all things and count them as rubbish, in order that I may gain Christ. (Phil. 3:7–8)

And:

> I will most gladly spend and be spent for your souls. (2 Cor. 12:15)

Through servant leadership and organizational commitment, leaders strive to remove their pride, their selfishness, and their and worldly aspirations. Servant leadership requires the leader to sacrifice his own self-interest and to be willing to die with Christ on the cross.[54] The Church needed to serve people to achieve her goal and mission. How can a church leader die with Christ on the cross, except in Baptism through daily repentance and contrition of heart?

Christ's death by crucifixion means that God's Son, Jesus Christ, had become incarnate as a man and came "to give His life as a ransom for many" (Matt. 20:28; Mark 10:45; 1 Tim. 2:6). While still hanging on the cross and facing imminent physical death, Jesus exclaimed, "τετέλεσται!" "It is finished!" (John 19:30). That is to say, "It is completed!" "It is accomplished!" "It is fulfilled!" "It is brought to the end!" "It is paid in full!"

Sin brings indebtedness or condemnation. The Law imposes an impossible indebtedness of performance before God. In the death of Jesus Christ on the cross, the debt is paid in full. There is no more condemnation. There are no more performance requirements.

God works through Baptism to give the treasure of faith, which receives the forgiveness of sins that Christ has won for us. Every Christian in and through Baptism is offered victory over death and the devil, forgiveness of sin, God's grace, the entire Christ, and the Holy Spirit with His gifts. Baptism is given by Christ in such a way that we derive strength and comfort from it when our sins or conscience oppress us.

From the benefits of Baptism, we can say that Baptism signifies that "the Old Adam in us should by daily contrition and repentance be drowned and die with all sins and evil desires, and that a new man should daily emerge and arise to live before God in righteousness and purity forever."[55] Paul writes: "We were buried therefore with Him by baptism into death, in order

---

[54] Paul T. P. Wong and Don Page, "Servant Leadership: An Opponent-Process Model and the Revised Servant Leadership Profile," in *Proceedings of the Servant Leadership Research Roundtable* (University Park, Penn.: Servant Leadership Research Roundtable, 2003), 13, http://citeseerx.ist.psu.edu/viewdoc/download?doi=10.1.1.714.6333&rep=rep1&type=pdf.

[55] Luther, *Luther's Small Catechism with Explanation*, 25.

that, just as Christ was raised from the dead by the glory of the Father, we too might walk in newness of life" (Rom. 6:4).

The entire life of a church leader is a life of trust in the promises of God offered in and through Holy Baptism. This life is constantly returning in prayers to Baptism in moments of temptation and suffering. The cross of Jesus is a "finished work." We cannot return there, but we can return to Christ in our Baptism. On the cross, we died with Jesus. In Baptism, God buried us and raised us with Him to a new life. A church leader walking in Baptism, therefore, produces and promotes faithful stewardship.

Effective leadership in the church is filled with purpose, opportunities, and relationships.[56] Leaders have countless roles and duties to accomplish daily. Effective leadership consists of many traits and behaviors. While effective leaders do exist, most professionals could not lead, and they do not want to be followed.[57]

True church leadership derives authority from a righteous example, not merely from prestige, personality, or position. Leadership is not about a system, but about character.[58] Some of the major traits of church leadership include intelligence, self-confidence, determination, integrity, and sociability.[59]

The word *integrity* is a word and notion commonly used in discussions of leadership and organizational theory but is not clearly defined or understood. Within the literature exploring types and systems of leadership, words such as *integrity*, *honesty*, and *conscientiousness* are often not distinguished; they are used interchangeably without commentary. Additionally, the word *integrity* is ingrained within the "moral relativist tradition" in which perceptions of appropriate behavior varies between peoples, cultures, and generations. Such relativism could be defensible in theory, but practically, this concept becomes problematic.[60] There is often a mismatch between the what

---

[56] Olga Epitropaki and Robin Martin, "Implicit Leadership Theories in Applied Settings: Factor Structure, Generalizability, and Stability over Time," *The Journal of Applied Psychology* 89, no. 2 (April 2004): 293.

[57] J. R. Fisher, "What Will It Take to Transform Your Organization in the 21st Century?" *Journal for Quality & Participation* 22, no. 6 (2009): 10.

[58] Mark L. McCaslin, "The Landscape of Leadership Building Relationships," *Journal of Leadership Studies* (September 14, 2016): 21, accessed February 25, 2019, https://journals.sagepub.com/doi/pdf/10.1177/107179190100800202.

[59] Stephen J. Zaccaro and Zachary N. J. Horn, "Leadership Theory and Practice: Fostering an Effective Symbiosis," *Leadership Quarterly* 14, no. 6 (December 2003): 110.

[60] Mark L. Rieke and Stephen J. Guastello, "Unresolved Issues in Honesty and Integrity Testing," *American Psychologist* 50, no. 6 (June 1995): 458.

leaders say and what they actually do. A leader may state that he has certain values, but they are not reflected in his behavior.[61]

Because stated values of leaders cannot alwasy be trusted, the focus in church leadership should be in Behavioral Integrity (BI). Behavioral Integrity is shorthand for behavior that is faithful to God's Word. The idea of BI is important because the positive organizational effects of integrity—such as the development of trust, increased commitment, and reciprocal respect—will mean nothing if actions of leaders don't follow what they espouse.[62] For an oganization to survive in the long-term, leadership and business practices must follow ethical and moral standards. The Ten Commandments were held in high esteem by Martin Luther as the true fountain from which all good works must flow when he said:

> Consider your place in life according to the Ten Commandments: Are you a father, mother, son, daughter, husband, wife, or worker? Have you been disobedient, unfaithful, or lazy? Have you been hot-tempered, rude, or quarrelsome? Have you hurt someone by your words or deeds? Have you stolen, been negligent, wasted anything, or done any harm?[63]

The Law of God is used by the Holy Spirit to teach us what sin is and what works are pleasing to God. His Word alone sets the standard for sin and for good works. Through the Ten Commandments, church leaders know and want to do good works and serve in their leadership effectively and efficiently.

2.2.5 Barriers to Effective Strengthening of Integrity and Accountability in Church Leadership

The reason why it is so important to strengthen proper biblical teaching concerning integrity is so that the church can hold leaders accountable.[64] Even though churches have been involved in social causes (such as the Civil Rights Movement, disaster relief, protection of children, support for the elderly, and helping the poor), church attendance has been declining in Christian churches.[65] Some scholars have researched this decline by asking those who left to explain their decision. The most frequent reasons are lack

[61] Simons, "Behavioral Integrity as a Critical Ingredient for Transformational Leadership," 101.

[62] Simons, "Behavioral Integrity as a Critical Ingredient for Transformational Leadership."

[63] Luther, *Luther's Small Catechism with Explanation*, 27.

[64] Rieke and Guastello, "Unresolved Issues in Honesty and Integrity Testing," 458.

[65] Robert Banks, *Reviewing Leadership: A Christian Evaluation of Current Approaches* (Grand Rapids: Baker Academic, 2004), 100.

of effective leadership, vision, and accountability in the leadership of the church.[66]

While there are many other reasons why organizations fail, the leader's lack of personal integrity, unfaithful and incompetent administration of his office, and lack of accountability are often key points of failure. The stronger an organization scores in servant leadership practices and leadership integrity when compared to tyrannical leadership practices, the healthier the organization.[67]

Certain indices are observed to inhibit effective strengthening of integrity and accountability in church leadership. These are:

1. **Defective beliefs and attitudes.** Many leaders believe that pocketing organizational funds makes them rich. They believe that having money is good, irrespective of the source. Hence some church leaders do not cease to support corrupt individuals. Church leaders and their leadership often do not question the source of wealth of members and followers whenever they donate bountifully to them. In addition, deeply held beliefs that corrupt people are intelligent or that corruption is an entitlement are a serious barrier to building resistance to corruption.[68] The work of civil society organizations (CSOs) and anti-corruption agencies in demanding accountability should increase. There is still much to do in order for churches to insist on accountability. Bringing about change in this area must be an important priority. Unfortunately, it becomes very difficult, perhaps, when the church leaders are involved.

   It is a form of thought and an activity of natural reason. A belief which is a form of human wisdom and reason can rise, judge, and conclude what it sees before its eyes or feel or apprehend with its senses. But faith is alive through the power of the Holy Spirit in the heart of a Christian leader. With faith, church leaders understand that Christ is in their soul to remove them from defective belief and bring them to true (divine) belief: "It is written, 'Man shall not live by bread alone, but by every word that comes from the mouth of God" (Matt. 4:4).

---

[66] Cathy Driscoll and Margaret McKee, "Restorying a Culture of Ethical and Spiritual Values: A Role for Leader Storytelling," *Journal of Business Ethics* 73, no. 2 (June 1, 2007): 209, https://doi.org/10.1007/s10551-006-9191-5.

[67] James A. Laub, "Organizational Health," *Servant Leader Performance*, n.d., 112, https://olagroup.com/Display.asp?Page=organizational_health.

[68] Cooper, "The Transformational Leadership of the Apostle Paul," 48.

2. **Ineffective accountability systems.** The issue of accountability is focused primarily on adherence to established regulations and legal requirements. Inadequate administrative oversight, decisions that fail to consider available resources, unwillingness to hold fully accountable those who are responsible for loss of church funds, corrupt practices that adjust to and influence new accountability systems are major concerns. It is challenging to ensure that religious norms and regulations are adhered to. For the sake of strengthening integrity, the church leadership must seek ways to enhance compliance.
3. **Lack of effective leadership and accountability.** Leadership is often corrupt when it is not fully accountable in matters of unrestricted procurement, recruitment and promotions, exercising of influence, use of funds, methods of obtaining loyalty, and the recording of financial records. When these areas are corrupted, the impact often leads to the view of corruption as being a part of normal or acceptable behavior in the vineyard of God. When roles overlap, misunderstandings and direct interference too often characterize the relationship between accounting officers and their leaders. These are areas that require clarification. This reality of "low standards in high places" is a fundamental issue to be addressed, primarily by the church leadership.
4. **Moral decay in the ministry.** Issues of getting rich quick become alarming in the ministry as seen in the life of some church leaders, and it has a direct relevance to corruption. Ministers of God who are in a position to withhold spiritual services in order to extract money from members and followers do so to gain additional income. They do these without taking cognizance of the fact that the church is not a business enterprise. They are mostly influenced by these behaviors to spiritualize all activities that have to do with their interaction with the members and followers, yet monetize also every spiritual event. Indeed, integrity cannot be strengthened in such a leader due to their nefarious operation in the service to God and lack of accountability in the leadership. At the same time, it is also clear that increase in wealth creation in the ministry would not on its own remove corruption.

   It is in this context that the overall education of the church leaders, including seminars, conferences, reorientation programs toward greater productivity, providing quality religious services, and ensuring accountability and value to strengthen their integrity coupled with their personality is central in ensuring a more effective means to curb the barriers. In such education, the ministry should be noted to involve the proclamation of the Gospel of Jesus in such a way that it is effective both on the local level and the church at large, whether we refer to Christ's own mission in this world or a number of different offices in His Church. Ministry is better understood in the context of ecclesiology as part of the teachings of the Holy Scriptures which the Confessions of the Church expound. Ministry is the creation of God by the Word for the Church. God offers the ministry to the Church as elect from all nations. The Church, therefore, is Christ's ambassador, proclaiming the Gospel and administering the Sacraments. "This is how one should regard us, as servants of Christ and stewards of the mysteries of God" (1 Cor 4:1).

The New Testament teaches that the office of the holy ministry refers to the shepherding of Christ's flock through the Means of Grace by men appointed by Jesus Christ through the call of the Church. Carefully understood, the ministry is not ruling and governing of the members and "followership" of the Church. It is concerned with serving. Thus it is a service of love. The ministry of the disciples was not grounded on any specific form of organization, on titles, privileges, rights, knowledge, or power, as in secular practices, but solely on the principle of serving their Master and His people. Christ by His example determined what the nature and essence of the church ministry would be when He washed His disciples' feet, saying: "I have given you an example, that you also should do just as I have done to you" (John 13:15).

Church leadership, whether as shepherding the flock of Christ in a congregation by a called servant of Christ (pastor) who administers the Word and Sacraments or service of loving concern for God and His people by apostles, bishops, teachers, prophets, deacons, deaconesses, evangelists, elders, pastors, and the like, is a service after Christ's mission—"As the Father has sent Me, even so I am sending you" (John 20:21).

The ministry of Christ's Church, then, exists for the purpose of saving sinners through the Gospel. Therefore, it is required that a called and ordained servant of the Word should be apt to teach and preach the Word in season and out of season, administer the Sacraments, forgive sins, and offer this service as a servant and not ruling over people like a secular leader.

2.2.6 Strategies That Strengthen Integrity and Accountability of Church Leaders

Accountability mostly refers to the establishment of a checks-and-balances system to protect organizations or group of individuals from harm within themselves and others. However, it is only church leaders with high integrity that make excellent candidates for leadership positions because they will not steal organizations' resources, treat others unfairly, or deceive themselves or others.[69] The Church and churchy organizations at their core hold to the biblical foundations of morality and ethical standards (the Ten Commandments and Golden Rule). Leaders in the church also recognize that all people are created in the Image of God and deserve the honor and respect that bestows despite race, tribe, social standing, philosophical or religious beliefs. All people should be accorded a basic human dignity because they were created by God Himself.

Theologically speaking, the church leader recognizes that all people are fallen creatures and have the same standing before God as sinful humans who need the forgiveness of Christ Jesus. This recognition allows the church leader to approach all people on equal footing. This is even more so for church leaders working with other Christians. This is the best strategy to strengthen their integrity in the vineyard of God.

Notably, these kinds of church leaders are best prepared for shepherding in the services to humanity which also is the service of the Lord. Nevertheless, they would be found to be ethical in their leadership in the church. Ethical leadership is the capacity of leaders to provide direction that enables the organization to fulfill its mission and vision as well as achieving declared goals.[70] In other words, a leader shepherds or guides people to achieve outcomes that the organization desires.

A leader's behavior varies depending on that individual's leadership style. Some of the ingredients that go into leadership style involve the personality of the leader. Some personality traits can be beneficial to leadership, while others are not as helpful—and a good leader tries to overcome or at least not negatively affect his leadership with them. Some leaders are very charismatic and seem to have the ability to mold people to their will and desires. Ethical, charismatic leaders use this ability to lead employees to achieve the goals of the organization. Unethical charismatic leaders abuse

---

[69] Becker, "Integrity in Organizations," 160.

[70] Olga Epitropaki and Robin Martin, "The Moderating Role of Individual Differences in the Relation between Transformational/Transactional Leadership Perceptions and Organizational Identification," *The Leadership Quarterly* 16, no. 4, Leadership, Self, and Identity (August 1, 2005): 589, accessed February 25, 2019, http://www.sciencedirect.com/science/article/pii/S1048984305000639.

their power to influence people for their own gain. Leaders are often more effective when they share the same values, beliefs, practices, and culture of the organization or institution. Organizations that seek a leader have the responsibility of identifying their values, beliefs, practices and culture so that they can find a good fit for a position.

When accountability is the watchword for the church leaders, they would initiate the cultural environment that tends to communicate discipline and amiable interpersonal relationships among church members. Common observations indicate that church leaders that demand quality service to the Lord in the church would tend to exhibit zero tolerance for corrupt practices. They would be inclined to promote quality service with integrity that can deliver value for money, accountability, and transparency in their attempt to lead others. This is because a society with integrity would cherish integrity. Demand for quality service can as well demand zero tolerance for corruption, cherish accountability, and be transparent in their leadership process.[71]

Hence church leaders who cherish integrity would institute initiatives to fight against corruption and reject the fiend in the leadership of the church. Thus they institute strategies that increase public awareness for accountability and enforce anti-corruption measures in church finance as well as other resources, protecting them from the hands of corrupt individuals or bad eggs.

---

[71] Bernard M. Bass, *Transformational Leadership*, 2nd ed. (Mahwah, N.J.: L. Erlbaum Associates, 2006), 13.

The following strategies are suggested to strengthen the integrity and accountability of church leaders:

Strategic objectives	Activity	Expected Outcome
Enhance church capacity in terms of standards and programs.	Church leaders should develop a training program such as seminars and workshops to educate on the need for accountability.	It is anticipated that this program, if successfully nurtured, would serve as an anti-corruption exercise that would remedy the church.
Strengthen anti-corruption planning, coordination, and implementation of church ethics.	This invites church leaders to discipline themselves, before setting up a disciplinary committee to check corrupt practice or embezzlement.	Accountability would be achieved in every facet of church leadership and administration when church leaders discipline themselves against fraud and mismanagement of economic resources of the church.
	Undertake financial, human resource, equipment, and logistic training to establish the departmental needs and offer assistance for future planning.	This would certainly make the leadership of the church effective.
	Strengthen records (financial and physical) and information management within the church information system.	This would improve the capacity to plan and manage financial, physical, and human resources in the church and cooperation among followers.
Support research program on policy development and implementation in conjunction with key church leaders.	Encourage research and write-ups that would publicize the church by way of sponsorship.	This would sensitize the people and the followers would become happy for their church to be known.
	Set committees and delicate responsibilities to others to be part of the church leadership.	It would engender leadership effectiveness as well as generate a positive perception of members to support the leadership wholeheartedly.

2.2.7 Church Leaders' Integrity and Members' Perception of Their Leadership Effectiveness

Integrity is required for any leader that wants to be effective in his service in the Church. Church members recognize the efforts of their leaders through the perception of their personality. Members of the church or any organization can only perceive their leaders' performance effectiveness if the leadership is honest with the people they are leading. Leaders need the integrity to function effectively.

Principle-centered leadership is the foundation of all leadership activities.[72] The extent to which principles and values of the organization are respected and adhered to is due to the understanding and recognition of integrity as a virtue. Remaining faithful to God's Word is a leader's first priority in spite of popular opinion, which may or may not support faithful decisions. Hence church leaders' integrity may have influences on members' perception of their leadership effectiveness, especially in Lutheran Church of Nigeria.

The Diamond of Managerial Integrity is a model which assesses and improves the integrity of managers[73] and explores the role of integrity in leading global companies. It states that "without integrity, managers of the organization will never engender the goodwill and trust of the organization, both essential for effective leadership."[74] As a concept of ethical leadership, church leaders need to be capable of promoting the interpersonal relationship between themselves and members of the church.[75] A leader who acts with integrity will make it more possible for members to regard their leader as effective.

---

[72] Covey, *Principle-Centered Leadership*, 15.

[73] Graeme Currie, Inger Boyett, and Olga Suhomlinova, "Transformational Leadership within Secondary Schools in England. A Panacea for Organizational Ills?," *Public Administration* 83, no. 2 (June 1, 2005): 265, accessed February 25, 2019, https://onlinelibrary.wiley.com/doi/abs/10.1111/j.0033-3298.2005.00450.x.

[74] Roseanne J. Foti and Carissa H. Luch, "The Influence of Individual Differences on the Perception and Categorization of Leaders," *The Leadership Quarterly* 3, no. 1 (March 1, 1992): 55, accessed February 25, 2019, http://www.sciencedirect.com/science/article/pii/1048984392900062.

[75] George B. Graen and Mary Uhl-Bien, "Relationship-Based Approach to Leadership: Development of Leader-Member Exchange (LMX) Theory of Leadership over 25 Years: Applying a Multi-Level Multi-Domain Perspective," *The Leadership Quarterly* 6, no. 2 (June 1, 1995): 219, accessed February 25, 2019, http://www.sciencedirect.com/science/article/pii/1048984395900365.

The concept of ethical leadership helps generate peace between the leaders and followers.[76] Leaders define not only the organizations strategy but especially the ethical climate and culture of the organization.

Ethical leadership is capable of streamlining church culture to foster the effective participation of members in church activities whereby church leaders would demonstrate caring attitudes and characteristics that motivate followers to perceive that their leadership is effective. Especially in the church, people do not desire job performance at any cost, but expect that the leader conducts his business in an ethical way. Job performance is connected with ethical behavior aligned with the values and goals of the organization. As a result, the ethical leader cares both for employees and shareholders in the organization.[77]

In considering job performance as that which is consistent with ethical values and principles, there are six distinct stages that, when properly applied, encourage Christians to strive to accomplish even more, simultaneously improving or strengthening their capacity and increasing their desire. The following section is based upon Lorin Woolfe's *The Bible on Leadership*:[78]

1. **The setting of goals.** Here church leaders help people determine ambitious yet realistic goals and motivate them toward completion. The Israelites believed in God's promise that they would someday be as numerous as the stars in the heaven. The apostles believed that someday their small group would grow to reach every corner of the world so that every race, tribe, and language would become part of God's kingdom. The Lord is faithful to his Old and New Testament promises for the Church.
2. **Inspiration.** The leader inspires his followers to accomplish the organization's goals. For example, Moses inspired the people of Israel to cross the desert to the edge of the Promised Land. Nehemiah, in the face of great opposition, inspired God's people to rebuild the wall around Jerusalem. Jesus called His disciples by calling them to become fishers of men (Mark 1:17).

   Leaders should be committed to the ultimate goals of the Church even when mistakes are made in the pursuit of the goal. Sometimes people feel disempowered and demotivated because of past mistakes.

[76] Nicholas M. Allix, "Transformational Leadership: Democratic or Despotic," *Educational Management & Administration* 28, no. 1 (January 1, 2000): 8.

[77] Graen and Uhl-Bien, "Relationship-Based Approach to Leadership," 224.

[78] Lorin Wolfe, *The Bible on Leadership: From Moses to Matthew—Management Lessons for Contemporary Leaders* (New York: American Management Association, 2002).

3. **Encouragement.** Encouragement means catching someone doing something right. It is the engine of excellent job performance. Many great projects started with heightened enthusiasm fizzle out due to lack of encouragement. In Heb. 3:13, the early Christians are urged to encourage one another daily. Reminding his followers, Paul says, "I did not shrink from declaring to you anything that was profitable" (Acts 20:20).

   Difficult tasks require ongoing encouragement. Barnabas, one of Jesus' disciples, was originally called Joseph, but he was given a new name that means "son of encouragement." *Encouragement* is rooted in the Latin for "heart" (*cor*). Moses encouraged the tribes of Israel by blessing them. Punishment and reproach discourages people, while blessing encourages people. This is built into our nature and is similar to the theological principle of Law and Gospel. God's Law kills the sinner, while the Gospel gives life and salvation.

   It is sad that many congregations of Lutheran Church of Nigeria and other Lutheran churches around the world are losing members because their leaders use harsh words from the pulpit and during church fellowship activities. Moses not only called the tribes to repentance by pointing out their sins and shortcomings, but he proclaimed the blessing of God upon them to remind them of God's favor and to encourage them. He said about Joseph:

   > Blessed by the Lord be his land, with the choicest gifts of heaven above, and of the deep that crouches beneath, with the choicest fruits of the sun and the rich yield of the months, with the finest produce of the ancient mountains and the abundance of the everlasting hills, with the best gifts of the earth and its fullness and the favor of Him who dwells in the bush. May these rest on the head of Joseph, on the pate of him who is prince among his brothers. (Deut. 33:13–16)

   Moses knew how powerful encouragement is to achieving important goals. When the desert sands looked unending, the Israelites cried out with hunger, and when internal dissidents threatened to undermine the goal of possessing the "land of milk and honey," crying out to return to Egypt, Moses reminded the Israelites that the land truly existed, even if they had not seen it. Church leaders often forget that people look up to hear the truth of how they are doing. We acknowledge how difficult this might be to do this in a gentle and positive manner.

4. **Discipline.** Discipline should be directed towards making the recipient feel motivated to improve bad behavior, not as punitive. Most people in the church will accept discipline that is fairly and justly administered. Jeremiah prayed for God to "correct me, O LORD, but in justice; not in Your anger" (Jer. 10:24).

   Church leaders are to guide very carefully how they react to those who depart from established orders or propose innovation. They should strive to show their accountability in every attempt to improve a bad behavior.

5. **Reward.** Something frequently forgotten by people is the importance for the leader to praise, encourage, and reward people for a job well done. In the desire to seek performance and accomplish results, it is easy to forget to reward or to acknowledge the good work done. A good leader rewards his people.

   In 1 Cor. 3:8 Paul states: "He who plants and he who waters are one, and each will receive his wages according to his labor." We can also look at Joshua's generosity toward his followers: the Reubenites, the Gadites, and the half-tribe of Manasseh—all of whom had helped him conquer the neighboring tribes:

   > "You have kept all that Moses the servant of the LORD commanded you and have obeyed my voice in all that I commanded you. You have not forsaken your brothers these many days, down to this day, but have been careful to keep the charge of the LORD your God. And now the LORD your God has given rest to your brothers, as He promised them. Therefore turn and go to your tents in the land where your possession lies, which Moses the servant of the LORD gave you on the other side of the Jordan." . . . So Joshua blessed them and sent them away, and they went to their tents. . . . And when Joshua sent them away to their homes and blessed them, he said to them, "Go back to your tents with much wealth and with very much livestock, with silver, gold, bronze, and iron, and with much clothing. Divide the spoil of your enemies with your brothers. (Josh. 22:2–8)

   There is power in positive rewards, even words of appreciation. Positive rewards develop loyalty and commitment to future performance.

6. **Firm But Fair Practices.** Combining structured, exacting behavior and performance with kindness and impartiality is a rare balance to achieve. However, leaders who are able to do so receive a high level of loyalty from their "followership" and

congregations. Woolfe notes that Scripture clearly draws up the stages of admonition in Matt. 18:15–17:

1. Confront negative behavior.
2. Give an opportunity to change.
3. End the relationship if there is no improvement (treat him as a pagan).

On the basis of Scripture, accountability and integrity can be strengthened in church leadership, reflecting thus:

1. "Sin no more, that nothing worse may happen to you" (John 5:14).
2. "I rejoice, not because you were grieved, but because you were grieved into repenting" (2 Cor. 7:9).
3. "I will discipline you in just measure. (Jer. 30:11).

Communication of performance expectations before, during, and after our tasks is very important. Therefore,

1. Set bold and realistic goals.
2. Offer rewards when a goal is obtained as encouragement.
3. No goal is achieved without risk and mistakes. Do not punish people for honest mistakes.
4. Celebrate collaborative efforts and accomplishment.
5. Like David and his mighty men, make members of congregations and followers feel like partners in the mission of the Church.
6. Christians pray that God will bless their efforts as they remain committed to being faithful to the Word of God, trusting the Holy Spirit to give success as He wills, even as they make plans and organize themselves for their work.

2.2.8 Accountability of Church Leaders and Members' Perception of Their Leadership Effectiveness

Good leaders will work in a loving, gentle, and kind manner and not demand obedience on the basis of the authority of their office. Working together, leaders and members of the organization therefore are able to meet the goals and objectives of the organization.[79] Hence church leaders' integrity may have influences on members' perception of their leadership effectiveness.

---

[79] S. M. Ngu, *Management Principles and Workers Motivation in Nigeria* (Zaria, Nigeria: Gaskiya Corporation Ltd, 2005), 12.

2.2.9 Church Leaders' Integrity and Their Members' Willingness to Follow ("Followership")

Great leaders have existed inside and outside of the church in world history. Great leaders are blessed by God with the gifts and talents they need as they continue to grow in their abilities to lead. We have touched on some of these qualities, such as integrity and commitment to principles and goals with the ability to rally people behind a cause. Although it does not happen often, there are times when a leader's unfailing commitment can even cause them personal harm and in some cases even the threat of death or death itself. These moments are defining for a leader and can propel someone from relative anonymity to being remembered as a great leader for all time. Leadership is sometimes thrust upon a person by the moment or the circumstance. It occurs when the person acts with integrity and stands firm to his principles. In the Church, we call this making a confession, resulting in the person becoming a witness or a martyr.

One example of a Christian leader thrust into the moment was Polycarp (AD 69–155), the Bishop of Smyrna. Church history says that Polycarp was a disciple of the apostle John. Polycarp was captured by those persecuting the church. Because of his age (perhaps late 80s), he was given an opportunity to recant and reject Jesus. *The Martyrdom of Polycarp* provides an account of what happened when Polycarp was given the opportunity to recant:

> And when he came near, the proconsul asked him whether he was Polycarp. On his confessing that he was, [the proconsul] sought to persuade him to deny [Christ], saying, Have respect to your old age, and other similar things, according to their custom, [such as], Swear by the fortune of Caesar; repent, and say, Away with the Atheists. But Polycarp, gazing with a stern countenance on all the multitude of the wicked heathen then in the stadium, and waving his hand towards them, while with groans he looked up to heaven, said, "Away with the Atheists." Then, the proconsul urging him, and saying, "Swear, and I will set you at liberty, reproach Christ'; Polycarp declared, "Eighty and six years have I served Him, and He never did me any injury: how then can I blaspheme my King and my Saviour?"[80]

Because Polycarp confessed Christ and remained with integrity, honor, and committed to his convictions, he was martyred by being burned at a stake. He lost his earthly life but gained a heavenly crown. His example of integrity inspired countless Christians as they were confronted with denying Christ and forsaking the integrity of their convictions. Polycarp was totally committed to his confession of Christ and to his convictions.

---

[80] *Martyrdom of Polycarp*, http://www.newadvent.org/fathers/0102.htm.

Great leaders remain committed to their principles. Integrity is not something faked, but it is observed by the people who follow the leader. Examples of leadership are not seen always when the event occurs. The followers of Polycarp probably never realized that his story would inspire generations of Christians. Martin Luther at the Diet of Worms in 1521 likely did not see his words before the Emperor, "Here I stand" as an example of leadership. His words, "Here I stand,"[81] have inspired Christians for the past 500 years, and are seen as an example of courage and leadership in the face of great pressure and difficulty. Luther kept his integrity even if it would mean his imprisonment or death. A leader's integrity is noticed by those who follow him; integrity helps build relationships with people.

Wendelin Küpers in his "Perspectives on Integrating Leadership and Followership"[82] develops a framework that shows the interconnection between leadership and peoples' willingness to follow. This model is helpful in visualizing different aspects of leadership. His model consists of four quadrants, with followership existing in the middle where all four quadrants meet. The first quadrant describes the personal aspects of the leader, his values, feelings, attitudes, etc. It reflects how he governs himself. Followership emerges when his inner or personal self manifests itself in externals that followers can see. In one sense, it is a genuineness test. Does the leader's personal and inner life match up with what people see?[83]

The second quadrant describes external traits people can measure in a leader, such as knowledge, skills, accountability, performance, etc. It also relates to the interaction between leaders and subordinates. In one sense, this quadrant reflects a skill set that might be found on a resume, or the practical qualifications for a position. A leader who does not have the necessary skills for a position will have difficulty retaining followers. At the same time, a qualified leader who lacks integrity or other aspects of the quadrants also will have difficulty retaining followers.[84]

The third quadrant deals with what is shared between leaders and followers in the organization. For instance, an organization has a history, a culture, internal rules, unwritten rules, a common worldview, shared experiences, etc. For example, a leader of a church or church organization who was a member from birth or a young age, who attended that church's schools, and who has been connected to it his entire life, may have more followers

---

[81] Concordia Publishing House, "Did Luther Really Say Here I Stand?", https://blog.cph.org/read/everyday-faith/lutheranism/did-luther-really-say-here-i-stand.

[82] Wendelin Küpers, "Perspectives on Integrating Leadership and Followership," https://www.regent.edu/acad/global/publications/ijls/new/vol2iss3/kupers/Kupers_Vol2Iss3.pdf

[83] Küpers, "Perspectives," 199–200.

[84] Küpers, "Perspectives," 200–201.

than an outsider who came in later in life or has only been a part of the group for a few years. Sometimes this can be viewed as a leader's loyalty to an organization.[85]

The fourth quadrant involves the external and formal processes of an organization. This includes things such as strategic planning, financial controls, policies, and rules, and how people relate to one another in the organization. For example, a leader who has everything else going for him but does not follow the financial controls will likely lose followers because people will suspect he has embezzled or wasted funds (even if that were not the case).[86]

This quadrant system is helpful in identifying various aspects of how leadership and followership interact with each other. In one sense, integrity flows through each quadrant: integrity and consistency between one's internal and external life; integrity related to a person's skills, abilities, and qualifications. In Africa, nearly every "bishop" has a "doctorate," which indicates qualifications. Unfortunately, many of these "doctor bishops" merely purchased their diplomas instead of attended school. There is an integrity of sharing a common history with a church or organization. And finally, integrity in dealing with organization rules, principles, and interactions with employees. So while this book does not make consistent use of Küper's quadrant analysis, it has used some of the principles to identify the importance of integrity as it relates to all aspects of leadership.

Members seem to be encouraged and cooperative when the church leaders exhibit a character as well as a personality that brings good interpersonal interactions between them. These good interpersonal interactions and relationships tend to promote leaders' integrity before their followers, coupled with making their followers in church respect the leadership. However, church leaders' integrity is beneficial only when leaders exhibit the following personality traits:

1. **Commitment.** The first virtue of a church leader's integrity that could enhance members' willingness to follow is a commitment to a purpose of the ministry. Commitment is unwavering and uncompromising in any leader that has a member's progress at heart. A leader's commitment in service endures suffering that can cause the leader to doubt or to be blamed unjustly or falsely, and can even lead to the rejection of the leader.

   Jesus' ministry has a strong foundation in commitment to goal accomplishment. His main goal was to show to sinful humanity the love of the Father. On one occasion, He told the disciples:

85 Küpers, "Perspectives," 201–2.

86 Küpers, "Perspectives," 202–4.

"This is My commandment, that you love one another as I have loved you. Greater love has no one than this, that someone lay down his life for his friends" (John 15:12–13).

Jesus further lays out the characteristics of His ministry in commitment to true servanthood in three of the Gospels:

1. "For even the Son of Man came not to be served but to serve, and to give His life as a ransom for many" (Mark 10:45).
2. "For I have come down from heaven, not to do My own will but the will of Him who sent Me" (John 6:38).
3. "For who is greater, one who reclines at table or one who serves? Is it not the one who reclines at table? But I am among you as the one who serves" (Luke 22:27).

2. **Trustworthiness.** Without trustworthiness, it is impossible to have effective leadership. As a virtue, trustworthiness refers to loyalty and truthfulness in the manner and way of doing things.[87] Leaders, who act consistently with integrity, develop relationships and engender trust from followers. This implies that trustworthiness in church leaders observed by members who follow them has an effect on the situation and the standard by which events of the church could be handled. As the leader enters into trusting relationships with his staff, his example teaches the same staff how to have trusting relationships with one another. In any relationship, the essence of trust is not in its bind, but in its bond. So church members are expecting their leader to be a person in whom they can put faith and trust to hold their hands rather than to be a person that they have to hold up.

   Church leaders in the service of the Lord must not only establish trusting relationships with staff, but they also must teach those employees who may not have experience trusting those they serve. In any relationship, the essence of trust is not in its bind, but in its bond. So church members are expecting their leader to be a person in whom they can put faith and trust to hold their hands rather than to be a person that they have to hold up.

   The zeal and deep concern by apostle Paul for the preservation of his converts to the end is his understanding that his apostolic work is an imitation of the ministry of Jesus and that the work must bear fruit to be presented on the day of the Lord.

[87] Wood, "Adventures of Difference in Leadership Studies," 11.

Paul knows himself to be a steward endowed with a gracious and powerful gift (1 Cor. 4:1; Rom. 1:5).

Every gift brings with it a corresponding responsibility: a responsibility to work, labor, and toil. Paul toils by preaching with an aim to present saints gathered on the Last Day before Christ, our Lord and Savior. However, his toil was not enough for him. It provided no reward until his congregations' faith, love, and generosity offered him the opportunity of testimony before others (2 Cor. 7:4, 14; 2 Thess. 1:4).

The toil, labor, and work of leadership in the Church are not done by the leader's own power, but by God's power at work in the Gospel through him. But it does not happen apart from the leader's own commitment, mirroring the divine love of Christ. Consider, for example, Nehemiah.

> No doubt Nehemiah possessed good leadership skills, some of which were God given and others that were learned through education and experience. Some of his administrative ability came from the training he had as a cupbearer in the Persian king's court. Once in Jerusalem, he was able to quickly assess the damage to the walls and formulate a plan to repair them. He also succeeded in uniting the community. . . . Nehemiah neither credited himself for the rebuilding of the walls, nor did he trust in his skill or leadership abilities. Instead, he recognized that the Lord brought about this accomplishment. God used Nehemiah, the high priest, the priests, and all the workers to rebuild the wall. God did not allow Israel's enemies to succeed. So, while Nehemiah and others played a role, the Lord received all the credit for rebuilding His city.[88]

A good leader shares earthly credit with those who help him in accomplishing a task while giving ultimate glory and honor to the Lord who used him as an instrument to accomplish the Lord's work in the Church.

Each leader entrusted with the responsibility of leading God's people is charged with a bond that unifies and affects the fullness and richness of their own life with God in the communion of saints.[89]

---

[88] Albert B. Collver, *Ezra and Nehemiah: The Lord Is Faithful*, God's Word for Today (St. Louis: Concordia, 2009), 112, 114.

[89] Jonathan F. Grothe, *Reclaiming Patterns of Pastoral Ministry: Jesus and Paul*, Concordia Scholarship Today (St. Louis: Concordia, 1988), 59.

3. **Wisdom.** Daniel Payne (quoted in *The Power of Followership*) noted that wisdom endows a person to know how to use power and to recognize that knowledge is only a tool for wisdom to use.[90] Leadership integrity uses wisdom to help strengthen people, systems, and institutions. Wisdom sees beyond the present—considering the past, present, and the future—to help guide the leader. Wisdom drives integrity.[91]

   Wisdom does the will of the Lord (Jer 8:8–9). Wisdom applies the abilities a leader has been given and imbibes the individual with responsibility to follow through.

   Leaders who are wise are nourished by the Word. Sometimes the power of knowledge is confused with wisdom. Wisdom is a gift of God and not the power to control people or to put people down.

4. **Responsibility.** A sense of responsibility that comes with power requires leaders to demonstrate character by acting reliably and consistently. Responsibility models excellence in a way others aspire to it.[92] Responsibility must be embodied and real since church leaders are seen as examples to their followers. Church leaders should recognize the fact that they are always faced with the duty to assist people in the difficult moments of their lives. When the work is done responsibly, every member is treated as an individual, whose sufferings and challenges are not the same as everyone else's and who deserves an individualized response.

   Every congregational member deserves from his pastor the ministration of the Word at every contact. Church leaders by their calling are to serve as keepers of their followers. But sin destroyed the divine relationship of trust and dependence between human beings and God and between human beings and their fellow humans. Consequently, fear, competition, and dominion in relationships are experienced in all aspects of human life. Christian leaders are their brother's keeper, holding out hope for restoration to God and peace with the rest of creation.

   Church leaders are responsible for the restoration of their followers to a right relationship to God, as His sons, thereby bringing to the entire creation hope of release from its bondage to

[90] Robert Earl Kelley, *The Power of Followership: How to Create Leaders People Want to Follow, and Followers Who Lead Themselves*, 1st ed. (New York: Doubleday, 2002), 111.

[91] Cooper, "The Transformational Leadership of the Apostle Paul," 48.

[92] Cooper, "The Transformational Leadership of the Apostle Paul," 48.

decay. Through the ministry of reconciliation, wholeness, unity, and harmony among God's people in the Church, responsible leadership bears fruit, and Christ, the Prince of peace, is imitated.

5. **Courage.** One is not necessarily born with courage, but one is born with the potential to exhibit it. Without courage, church leaders cannot practice any other virtue with consistency. This is most likely because one cannot be kind, true, merciful, generous, or honest without courage. Church leaders need the courage to confront the overwhelming issues in the work of God that hinge on life and death. Church leaders should also know that they would be called upon to confront issues that affect their fair and respectful treatment of members and followers of God.
6. **Competency.** The common phrase says, "Knowledge is power." In reality, knowledge is only potential power that becomes power when used or abused.[93] Leaders, who lead with integrity, are not afraid to admit ignorance. However, a leader who has integrity brings proficiency and expertise to their work. They do not pretend to have knowledge or competency in areas they do not. Often knowledge is demonstrated by various leadership skills, academic learning, and experience. A church leader will be challenged to demonstrate knowledge and competency as well as encourage others to achieve competency in their tasks. This is another way a leader can lead by example, which inspires others to seek competency.
7. **Sensitivity.** Sensitivity helps others to feel strong physically, emotionally, and spiritually in their respective department of the ministry. Church leaders may be tempted to exhibit their power, but leaders who have integrity have the ability to consider the needs and feelings of other people.[94] Respect for the neighbor engenders sensitivity to and empathy for others and their needs. Consequently, respect for human lives must be at the core of one's conduct. What should be natural for the person in service to God and the church can be lost when empathy for others is lost and the focus becomes the self. This can result in the leader turning narcissistic. Church leadership is not an independent activity of exerting power and control, but one that relies on relationships with God and between people.

---

[93] Bass, *Transformational Leadership*, 12.

[94] Kelley, *The Power of Followership*, 111.

8. **Justice.** Church leaders are not appointed judges, but they judge issues affecting people rightfully with honest scriptural principles. They should realize that their leadership is singularly focused on the goal of the ministry of Christ. Church leaders should always take notice that whatever affects members or followers directly affects all indirectly. Sometimes justice is associated with entitlement, giving an individual what is due. Justice belongs to integrity as it allows one to consider the needs of an individual, even if it is not strictly owed to him.[95] Integrity in justice requires patience, wisdom, and empathy for an individual.
9. **Service.** Leaders with integrity do not seek their own glory or praise. They are not tyrants. Instead, they recognize that true greatness is found in humility. They serve Christ who humbled Himself to death on a cross (Phil. 2:8). Leaders, who have integrity, do not see themselves as superior because of their position. They actively help and enable those they lead to achieve success, recognizing that the success of their subordinates reflects well on them. The welfare of the people who work for them and of the organization is the priority, not power and prestige for one's self.
10. **Self-respect.** The leader who has self-respect recognizes his own value and worth. The leader is not a narcissist who uses other people to make himself feel better about himself or to create a false self worth. Self-respect allows the leader to discriminate the truth, love others, and remain objective. A leader who lacks self-respect is in danger of narcissistic behaviors, unable to love others or remain objective.

Integrity is practiced and developed. Both the actions and inactions of a leader determine his integrity. Leaders possessing integrity add virtues into their daily activities. They live honestly, being reliable and resourceful while expressing consideration for others. Leaders with integrity inspire and encourage others to greater levels of success. Leaders with integrity do not demand loyalty oaths, but are thankful when people demonstrate loyalty because of their leadership. Integrity accepts the weakness of others and accepts them regardless because of their value as human beings.

---

[95] Kelley, *The Power of Followership*, 111.

2.2.10 Church Leaders' Accountability and Members' "Followership"

"Followership" depends on the ability of a leader to exhibit behaviors that are lacking in other leaders. This becomes extrinsic motivation for any other human being to follow such a man as they do Christ. It could be reasoned that personality plays a significant role. That is why, in the church, leadership is vital to "followership," and the leader who leads is able to convince people in the society to rally around such ministry.

A leader is a person who manages a process toward the accomplishment of goals through the use of some person or group.[96] Thus showing the qualities of leadership is necessary for a team. The leader is seen as a head whose vision is to depend heavily on the formal authority of the office to ensure obedience from members of the organization.[97]

Leadership in the church specifically involves a series of vital roles such as teaching, counseling, discipline, policy implementation and coordination, recruitment of staff and retirement of staff for the growth of the organization.[98] Some people follow a man who is disciplined. Others follow a man who can teach and express himself fluently. Still others follow a man who has the ability to coordinate, organize, and even recruit. "Followership" is a concept worth discussing because it has dimensions of application in the ministry of God.

Some people followed Christ because He could heal. Others followed Him because they would eat well (cf. John 6). Still others followed Christ just to identify with Him and belong to His group. Jesus drew people to Himself because of His great compassion, evident to all, and the fact that He taught them with great authority as He proclaimed the Good News of the kingdom of God. Good leaders model themselves after the example of Christ. In a real sense, they presume to have followers and they need followers. This is because without the follower, the concept, ideals, spiritual skills, leadership potentials would not be known or recognized. It is presumably noted that personality traits have a significant effect on the "followership" and memberships in the heavenly business of Christ.

Church leaders must be held accountable by the Church for being and remaining faithful to God's Word as they demonstrate appropriate personalities and character traits. Without adequate personal accountability, leaders can easily fall into the temptation of being dishonest. Accountability

[96] J. C. Atado, *The Leader We Want* (Kano, Nigeria: Modern Printers, 2011) 112.

[97] Ngu, *Management Principles and Workers Motivation in Nigeria*, 12.

[98] Okoronta, "The Impact of Leadership Styles in the Pentecostal Churches on the Growth of the Gospel in Kaduna State," 15.

is determined by the level of transparency exhibited by the church leaders to an extent that church leaders are faithful, whether to the financial, material, and/or spiritual standards (confessions and teachings) of the church. When a church does not have in place administrative processes that make church leaders' salary matters of public knowledge, it encourages suspicion and complaints within the church.

An estimated $16 billion was embezzled in the year 2000 alone and $75 billion between 1980 and 2000 from the world's Christian churches.[99] Christians need to hold their leaders and their churches and organizations accountable (which in many cases they do by withholding funds or reducing gifts). They need to ask and consider how funds are used and insist upon control systems that utilize the strictest procedures. Some Christian organizations have excellent accountability in the collection and expending of funds. These leaders, churches, and organizations recognize that they are merely stewards of the gifts God has bestowed upon them by His people who make personal sacrifices of time, gifts, and skills for God's kingdom.

Members' "followership" seems to be encouraging and cooperating when the church leaders exhibit characteristics as well as a personality that bring good interpersonal interactions between them. This good interpersonal interactions and relationships tend to promote a leader's integrity before their followers, coupled with making their followers in church respect the leadership.

Mainline denominations in the West are in sharp decline[100] and have fallen into great disrespect in Africa due to their promotion of "social issues," such as homosexuality, abortion, etc., as well as neglecting the Gospel in favor of a whole host of other causes: environmentalism, politics, economics. The Church is called to remain faithful to God's Word and leave growth to the blessing of God, when and where He chooses to give it. Changing demographics in the West, as well as a lack of leadership and vision, along with the failure to communicate how the church impacts the world, are contributing to the decline. The church in the West also is failing to reach the

---

[99] David B. Barrett, George Thomas Kurian, and Todd M. Johnson, *World Christian Encyclopedia: A Comparative Survey of Churches and Religions in the Modern World*, 2nd ed. (Oxford: Oxford University Press, 2001), 1:11.

[100] Steve Bruce, "Secularisation, Church and Popular Religion," *The Journal of Ecclesiastical History* 62, no. 3 (July 2011): 543; Peter G. Coleman, Christine Ivani-Chalian, and Maureen Robinson, "Religious Attitudes among British Older People: Stability and Change in a 20-Year Longitudinal Study," *Ageing & Society* 24, no. 2 (2004): 172; Craig. Van Gelder, ed., *The Missional Church and Leadership Formation: Helping Congregations Develop Leadership Capacity*, Missional Church Series (Grand Rapids: Eerdmans, 2009).

youth.[101] The lack of leadership in the West has resulted in the decline of many organizations and church bodies.

Stronger organizations and church bodies practice servant leadership instead of a paternalistic or autocratic leadership model.[102] The most effective organizations practice a servant leadership style.[103]

2.2.11 Church Leaders' Integrity and People's Membership in the Church

The challenge to act upon our most dearly held beliefs and values confronts us all. A common problem in leadership occurs when there is a gap between what is professed and believed, and what is done. This can be expressed with the common axiom: do what I say, not what I do. Some have called this the "integrity gap." It is a recurring challenge for people to have the courage to practice what they preach, to do what integrity demands.[104]

Ethical conduct in leadership, trusting relationships with church leaders, and peoples' membership in the church or a family are prerequisites for healthy social environments. An ethical leader takes into account the concerns and issues of all the people. Such leadership is essential for the well-being of an organization.[105]

Of course, structures are not static. They are enfolded and entangled in each other.[106] Membership is pertinent to leadership because without membership there is no leadership in the church. Peoples' membership in the church seems to be encouraging and satisfying when the church leaders exhibit good interpersonal interactions. Good interpersonal interactions and relationships tend to promote leaders' integrity before their members, coupled with making their members in the church respect the church leadership as well as the leaders.

Often leaders are pressured by their corporate executive functions, working to increase the profitability of their corporations while trying to maintain ethical values, such as principled risk-taking and conventional decision-making. The following three areas should be considered:

---

[101] Driscoll and McKee, "Restorying a Culture of Ethical and Spiritual Values," 208.

[102] Laub, "Organizational Health," 113.

[103] Dorothy O. Potter, "The Traits/Characteristics, Attitudes, and Effective Work Environments of Servant Leaders: A Delphi Study" (PhD, Capella University, 2009), http://search.proquest.com/docview/305160274/abstract/344013EF0894095PQ/1.

[104] M. David Albritton, Sharon L. Oswald, and Joseph S. Anderson, "Leadership Quality and Follower Affect: A Study of U. S. Presidential Candidates," *Journal of Leadership Studies* 1, no. 4 (2008): 8, https://onlinelibrary.wiley.com/doi/abs/10.1002/jls.20035.

[105] Eighinger, *Condensed Version of the Study of Ethics.*

[106] Cooper, "The Transformational Leadership of the Apostle Paul," 48.

1. **Self-consistency, wholeness, or compartmentalization.** Do people think their beliefs apply at home, work, and in volunteer positions such as church? A consistency of internal beliefs with external actions that people can see matters.
2. **Personal.** Do people believe they have the power and ability to express and take action on their beliefs? People may hold certain beliefs but may feel powerless to express them externally.
3. **The scope of awareness.** Do people feel that they are responsible only for their own lives or do they believe that their actions have an impact beyond themselves and into the world?[107]

Leaders are rare persons who are not solely "principled risk-takers" or "conventional decision-makers." Most people are not solely risk-takers or solely conventional decision makers, but rather some combination. Examining the three areas above can help a person determine his capacity to be a leader in the face of the pressures and challenges a leader will confront. For instance, when a leader is confronted with pressure, will he take the easy way out by making people happy, or do things the way they have always been done?

The integrity church leaders should exhibit between church activities and their personal life may have an enduring effect on peoples' membership in the church. The integrity of the church's leaders is essential for the work of the church. A lack of integrity and accountability can destroy a church and cause it to abandon its commitment to the Gospel. It has a lot to do with the personality of the leaders and the leadership of the church.

2.2.12 Church Leaders' Accountability and People's Membership in the Church

Leadership remains a fundamental process in every organization.[108] The subject of leadership has captured many people's attention as a solution for everything in the church that is not well in order.[109] The characteristics or personality traits embedded in individual church leaders to some extent must be employed with some elements of accountability. A church that does not have a well-documented process for holding its leaders accountable encourages a culture of dishonesty and corruption.

Accountability is displayed by the transparency exhibited by the church leaders. It demonstrates the extent that church leaders are faithful

[107] Albritton, Oswald, and Anderson, "Leadership Quality and Follower Affect," 17.

[108] Okoronta, "The Impact of Leadership Styles in the Pentecostal Churches on the Growth of the Gospel in Kaduna State," 16.

[109] Strudler and Warren, "Authority, Heuristics, and the Structure of Excuses."

to the financial, material, and immaterial property of the church. Although some Christian organizations have excellent reputations regarding their accountability and use of funds in general, particularly in the Global South, Christians need to increase accountability and demand safeguards and controls on all funds.

It is acknowledged that leaders often have influence not just because they are experienced but because their leadership styles are a perfect fit for the ministry needs of an organization.[110]

2.2.13 Age and Church Leaders' Integrity

The age of a leader is suspected to have an effect on the leadership style and strategy, administration, and the integrity of such a leader. This is most often revealed in the pattern of discussions and interactions with others, such as church members and followers toward the affairs of God. This age factor is seen to have a relationship with the type and quality of experiences such a leader may possess.

The age of the staff can have an effect. Often older, more traditional staff came into church work from secular fields that had higher standards or greater accountability in general. Meanwhile, younger staff who entered church service via church mechanisms without the same experience as people in the secular world may not recognize the importance of those skills. This can create a dynamic where the younger workers do not value the concerns of the older staff who had more experience in the secular world.

The older church leaders claimed they were trained by first-line supervisors who in some instances could be several years older than the younger ones. The dynamics of the training differs from what is going on now; then that is added to the years of experience. Specifically, the older leaders seem to be uncomfortable with newcomers who joined the ministry at a younger age.

Discipline comes with the ability of leaders who often deal with a high intensity of emotional experiences in their interaction and relationship with others. To demonstrate disciplined behaviors in the vineyard of God, church leaders need tolerance. Tolerance might allow church leaders to connect, communicate, and understand their younger, less-experienced leader in the Gospel of Christ.

2.2.14 Age and Church Leaders' Accountability

A major factor in workplace dynamics is the age and experience of the people. Each generation's motivations and core values shift dramatically

[110] Bill Hybels, *Courageous Leadership* (Grand Rapids: Zondervan, 2002), 12.

from one age group to another.[111] The primary motivation to rationally thinking leaders is to give back and to serve, to do good for others depends on their age relative to the stages of psycho-social theory of development, thus certain actions performed and personality exhibited is due to age.

The following section draws on thoughts found from Dr. Richard Krejcir's article, "Understanding and Developing Christian Accountability."[112] In religious perspective, accountability is looked at as being open to what we are thinking and doing in order to receive encouragement and/or reproof.[113] Among others, Matt. 12:36; Rom. 2:16; 1 Cor. 3:10–15 recount that leaders are liable, responsible, and answerable to God for their actions in life. We hold leaders accountable to make sure they are fulfilling their duties.

Accountability could allow church leaders to be answerable to one another, focusing and discussing key relationships, such as those with their spouse, friends, peers, co-workers in the church, small department or group members, and other officials in the fold of Christ. This supposes the capacity of church leaders to be accountable for their actions and understand where they need help and support in areas where they are weak and struggling, where and how they are growing, what they are learning, and to be encouraged.

2.3 Summary of the Literature Review

This study's aim is to assess ways of strengthening integrity and accountability in the leadership of Lutheran church bodies, particularly in Africa. Theoretically, the literature review (chapter 2) showed that sociological investigation of the relationship between religion and class can generally be divided into: (1) those treating religion primarily as a dependent variable and (2) those treating it mainly as an independent variable and conflict rooted in philosophical materialism. The administration of an organization is always more efficient and effective when it holds itself accountable to clearly defined goals with accompanying action plans to achieve the goals. Leadership includes the ability to influence, motivate, guide, direct, and inspire people.

The review also demonstrated that followers will be more committed to being a part of the organization's mission, and achieving its goals, when their leaders are known to be persons of integrity and are being held accountable to clear standards and expectations. Leadership was also seen as a process

---

[111] Hybels, *Courageous Leadership*, 12.

[112] Richard Krejcir, "Understanding and Developing Christian Accountability," *Into Thy Word*, http://www.intothyword.org/apps/articles/default.asp?articleid=32243&blogid=0&fldAuthor=&fldKeywords=&fldTopic=0&link=1&url=10&view=post.

[113] Fry, Vitucci, and Cedillo, "Spiritual Leadership and Army Transformation," 862.

of influencing others to act and to accomplish a specific goal, consisting of interpersonal influence exercised in a situation and directing by means of communication processes the attainment of specified goals.

In addition, elements of dishonesty and nonaccountability in church leadership imply pretense and high level of dishonest behaviors exhibited by the leadership. Dishonesty factors and nonaccountability in church leadership is determined by the deliberate refusal to establish a checks-and-balances system to protect organizations or groups of individuals from harm within and to protect others because it is the responsibility of leaders to perform, conduct, and ascertain modalities that would be ideal for that purpose.

The review also showed the barriers to effective strengthening of integrity and accountability in the leadership are caused by an organization's style of leadership and a leader's integrity, as well as willingness to be honestly accountable. They are also created by defective beliefs and attitudes, ineffective accountability systems, lack of effective leadership and accountability, and moral decay in the ministry.

The strategies that strengthen the integrity and accountability of church leaders were studied also as accountability which could allow church leaders to be answerable to one another, focusing on key relationships as well as to be answerable to spouses, close friends, colleagues, co-workers in the church, small department or group members, and other officials in the fold of Christ.

A church leader's integrity was also determined to have an influence on the perception of members of the effectiveness of their leaders as it is considered a normative practice for any leader who has integrity in the midst of church membership. A church leader's integrity and a member's "followership" is recognized in hindsight, after the event is over.

CHAPTER THREE

RESEARCH METHODOLOGY

3.1 Design of the Study

This study adopted a survey design because it focuses on the examination of ways to strengthen integrity and accountability in the leadership of Lutheran Church of Nigeria. Even though the study focused on Lutheran Church of Nigeria, it has broader application to other Lutheran church bodies. This design was relevant to the study because it enabled the researcher to collect data from the respondents on their perception of the integrity of the leaders in Lutheran Church of Nigeria, their perception of their leadership effectiveness, accountability of the leaders in Lutheran Church of Nigeria, members' followership, membership in the church, and the age of the leaders. Others factors examined were elements of dishonesty and nonaccountability found in some leaders in Lutheran Church of Nigeria, possible factors that bring about dishonesty and nonaccountability among leaders, intent behind and the purpose of integrity- and accountability-strengthening policies, barriers to effective strengthening of integrity and accountability, and strategies that can help strengthen the integrity and accountability of church leaders in Nigeria. Readers, while studying the particular situation in Nigeria, should consider applications and examples in their own church body or other church bodies. It also provides an example on how one could conduct a similar study in another world region.

3.2 Area of the Study

The study area for this research was South-South Geo-Political Zone of Nigeria.[1] It comprises six states: Akwa Ibom, Bayelsa, Cross River, Delta, Edo, and Rivers states. It is strategically located at the point where the Y-tail of the river Niger joins the Atlantic Ocean through the Gulf of Guinea.

[1] There are only so many ways to describe the geography of a place. Many excellent online resources provide good descriptions. Please see *My Guide Nigeria*: https://www.myguidenigeria.com/regionalinfo/south-south-region.

Although a relatively small stretch of land, the south of the country provides the fuel for the Nigerian economy: oil. In addition to oil and gas, the region equally contributes other key resources, with the potential for huge investment opportunities in tourism and agriculture.

3.2.1 Akwa-Ibom State: Promised Land

Akwa-Ibom is located in the coastal part of the country, with an area of 7,081 square kilometers and a population of almost five million. The state shares boundaries with Cross River State, Rivers State, Abia State, and the Atlantic Ocean, with Uyo as its capital city. The main languages in the state are Ibibio, Annang, Eket, and Oron. Akwa-Ibom has a rich historical and cultural heritage with major attractions such as the Ibeno Sand Beach, Oron Museum, Mary Slessor House and monument tomb. Akwa-Ibom State is the third-largest producer of crude oil in the country and is endowed with various resources such as natural gas, salt, silver nitrate, limestone, clay, coal, and glass sand.

3.2.2 Bayelsa State: Pride of the Nation

Bayelsa is located in the lower southern part of the Niger Delta region, and its capital is Yenagoa. This state is blessed with many historical sites, such as the Slave Transit Hall, and cultural festivals (Ekpetiama Okelede new yam festival, Odemimon festival, Otuoke, and others), and it houses a population of two million people occupying an area of 10,773 square kilometers. There are ten languages spoken in the state; of these, Izon, Nembe, Ogbia, and Epie-Atissa are the most predominant. Bayelsa State, a major oil- and gas-producing area, accounts for more than 30 percent of Nigeria's oil production and is also renowned for fishing, farming, trading, carving, and weaving. With the majority of the state under sea level, more than three-quarters of the area is covered by water and consists of a maze of meandering creeks and mangrove swamps. In addition, Bayelsa has large reserves of clay, sand, and gravel which are of utmost importance to the industrial sector.

3.2.3 Cross River State: The People's Paradise

Calabar is the capital city of Cross River State. Being a coastal state, it shares boundaries with Benue State to the west, Abia State to the south and the Atlantic Ocean to the east. The major languages spoken in Cross River State are Ejagham and Efik. Cross River State is home to some of Nigeria's most beautiful scenery. More than half the land is covered by tropical rainforests, making it one of the world's biodiversity hot spots. The state is also blessed with natural resources such as oil and gas, limestone, kaolin, clay, salt, barite, and quartzite.

3.2.4 Delta State: The Big Heart

Delta State has Asaba as its capital and is made up of twenty-five local government areas. There are various solid mineral deposits in the state which include crude oil, industrial clay, silica, lignite, kaolin, tar sand, decorative rocks, and limestone, with many serving as raw materials for industries. Some major tourist attractions include Nana's Palace, Koko, Asaba Beach, Abraka River Resort Motel, and River Ethiope. There are also traditional festivals in every community: the Ishe Festival for peace and progress in Ewulu town; the Edjenu of the Agbarha Clan, which takes place only once or twice in a person's lifetime; and the Oki Masquerade of Torugbene.

3.2.5 Edo State: Heartbeat of Nigeria

Benin City is the capital of Edo State. The state is endowed with abundant natural resources of crude oil, clay, chalk, marble, natural gas, and limestone. Edo is home to several ethnicities with eighteen local government areas. There are many tourist attractions in the state: Oba's Palace in Benin City, Ramat Park, Sakpoba Holiday Resort, the Emotan statue in Benin City, Ishe Lake, and River Niger Beach in Agenebode, among others. There are more than one hundred major festivals celebrated in Edo State between September and March annually.

3.2.6 Rivers State: Treasure Base of the Nation

Port Harcourt is a cosmopolitan city and capital of Rivers State, which makes it the second largest commercial center in Nigeria. Rivers State boasts a diverse ethnic population of more than six million people and occupies an area of 11,077 square kilometers. The major languages are Ijaw and Ikwere, although twenty-three languages are spoken altogether. Rivers State accounts for more than 40 percent of Nigeria's crude oil production and food production—no wonder it's called the "treasure base of the nation." In addition, there are two major refineries and seaports in Rivers State, with various industries spread across it.

This study area (South-South Geo-Political Zone of Nigeria) was used by the researcher because it is a familiar area to me, and my state of origin is one of the states contained in it, making the proximity favorable to me by reducing the cost of having to travel long distances. Besides, in the six geopolitical zones in Nigeria, we have Lutheran Church of Nigeria.

3.3 The Population of the Study

The population of this study is comprised of all of the 404 officeholders and workers of Lutheran Church of Nigeria in South-South Geo-Political

Zone in Nigeria. They are members of LCN Board of Directors, members of LCN zonal boards, members of LCN district boards, LCN church councillors, LCN seminary faculty members, LCN Schools Management board members, principals of the Lutheran high schools, past presidents of LCN, past vice presidents of LCN, past district chairmen-lay, other workers of the church, and the entire congregation.

3.4 Sample and Sampling Technique

The sample of this study was 364 respondents, which was 90 percent of the target population. The sample size was determined statistically using "sample as a fraction" as a formula for the finite population.[2] The stratification was based essentially on local government area. In each of the stratum, simple random sampling techniques, using the hat and draw (balloting) method, selected the sample. In this technique, every member of the population has equal and independent opportunity of being selected, thereby achieving a representative sample. The researcher wrote the names of all the respondents in each local government area on a slip of paper, rolled each slip in a container (hat), and blindly drew the required number of personnel names in each of the local government areas. In the same manner, all the required samples were randomly drawn for the study. The sample size of 364 respondents who returned the questionnaire formed 90 percent of the study population of 404, while 348 respondents correctly and completely filled in their questionnaires. Hence, 348 questionnaires were used for the study, and it proved adequate to represent the study population.

3.5 Research Instrument

The instrument used for data collection in this study was a research questionnaire titled "Integrity and Accountability Strengthening in Church Leadership Questionnaire (IASCLQ)." The questionnaire was made up of two sections. Section A contained the demographic data of the respondents, such as name of the respondents, address of the church, gender, age, and position. Section B contained items on the main variables, such as perception of the integrity of the leaders, perception of leadership effectiveness, perception of accountability of the leaders, level of members' leadership and "followership," elements of dishonesty and nonaccountability, possible factors that bring about dishonesty and nonaccountability, intent behind and the purpose of integrity and accountability strengthening, the barriers to effective strengthening of integrity and accountability, the strategies that

[2] U. A. Ibanga, *Statistics for Social Sciences* (Jos, Nigeria: Centre for Development Studies, University of Jos, 1992), 12.

can help strengthen the integrity and accountability of church leaders. These variables will be measured each with five items.

3.6 Validity of the Research Instrument

The instrument was subjected to face validation by three experts. It was validated by two experts from the Department of Vocational Education, and one expert from Test and Measurement Department, University of Uyo. Their inputs were used to modify and streamline the instrument.

3.7 Reliability of the Instrument

The reliability study was conducted using forty respondents from members of Lutheran Church of Nigeria in South West Zone (i.e., Lagos State). Cronbach's Alpha technique was used to determine the reliability coefficient (0.89) of the instrument and proved the instrument reliable for use in the study.

3.8 Method of Data Collection

The researcher administered the questionnaire with the help of research assistants in many of the congregations visited. Retrieval of the questionnaire was done three days after the administration from each respondent. Before the exercise, the research assistants were trained on the administration of the research instrument. The researcher, from the onset, gave an introductory letter to the leaders of each congregation. This was done accordingly, and cooperation was expected from the assistants and respondents in the area of administration and retrieval of the questionnaire such that an assistant from each congregation was assigned to the research team in order to help identify the respondents, administer, and retrieve the questionnaires without the problem of mistaken identity.

3.9 Method for Data Analysis

The data was analyzed and the hypotheses tested using appropriate statistics, such as Regression Analysis and independent t-test analysis at 0.05 alpha levels. Regression Analysis is always used for prediction of the level of dependent variables using the power of the independent variables. In like manner for this work, the Regression Analysis was adopted in order to help predict the status of all the dependent variables by all the independent variables. Independent t-test analysis was used to compare the mean score of two independent groups. For this work, the independent t-test was used to compare the level of accountability of the older and younger leaders. Dependent t-test analysis was always used to compare the means between two related groups on the same continuous data of the dependent variable. For this work, dependent t-test was used to compare the level of integrity before and after teaching.

Decision Rule

The null hypothesis was retained where the calculated value was less than the critical value but rejected where the calculated value was either greater than or equal to the critical value.

CHAPTER FOUR

DATA ANALYSIS, RESULTS, AND DISCUSSION OF FINDINGS

4.1 Data Analyses and Results[1]

4.1.1 Hypothesis One

The null hypothesis states that there is no significant relationship between the integrity of the leaders in Lutheran Church of Nigeria and members' perception of their leadership effectiveness. In order to test the hypothesis, regression analysis was performed on the data (see Table 1).

Table 1. Regression Analysis of the Relationship between the Integrity of the Leaders in Lutheran Church of Nigeria and Members' Perception of Their Leadership Effectiveness

Model	R	R-Square	Adjusted R-Square	Std. the Error of the Estimate	R-Square Change
1	0.98*	0.96	0.96	0.32	0.96

*Significant at 0.05 level; df = 346; N = 348; critical R-value = 0.113

The table shows that the calculated R-value 0.98 was greater than the critical R-value of 0.113 at 0.5 alpha level with 346 degrees of freedom. The R-Square value of 0.96 predicts 96 percent of the association between the integrity of the leaders in Lutheran Church of Nigeria and members' perception of their leadership effectiveness.

[1] The methodology followed here is based upon the methodology used in Michael Nnamseh and Isaac Ayandele, "Effect of Employee Participation in Decision Making on Corporate Performance: A Case of Selected Banks in South-South Nigeria," *International Journal of Management Sciences* 7, no. 7 (2016): 350–58.

It was also deemed necessary to find out the extent of the variance of each case of the independent variable (integrity of the leaders in Lutheran Church of Nigeria and members' perception of their leadership effectiveness) as responded by each respondent (see Table 2).

Table 2. Analysis of Variance of the Relationship between the Integrity of the Leaders in Lutheran Church of Nigeria and Members' Perception of Their Leadership Effectiveness

Model	Sum of Squares	Df	Mean Square	F	Sig.
Regression	862.62	1	862.62	8298.04	0.000b
Residual	35.97	346	0.10		
Total	898.59	347			

The above table presents the calculated F-value as (8298.04) and the P-value as (.000). Being that the P-value (.000) is below the probability level of 0.05, the result, therefore, means that there is a significant relationship between the integrity of the leaders in Lutheran Church of Nigeria and members' perception of their leadership effectiveness

4.1.2 Hypothesis Two

The null hypothesis states that there is no significant relationship between accountability of the leaders in Lutheran Church of Nigeria and members' perception of their leadership effectiveness. In order to test the hypothesis, regression analysis was performed on the data (see Table 3).

Table 3. Regression Analysis of the Relationship between Accountability of the Leaders in Lutheran Church of Nigeria and Members' Perception of Their Leadership Effectiveness

Model	R	R-Square	Adjusted R-Square	Std. the Error of the Estimate	R-Square Change
1	0.96*	0.92	0.92	0.456	0.92

*Significant at 0.05 level; df = 346; N = 348; critical R-value = 0.113

The table shows that the calculated R-value 0.96 was greater than the critical R-value of 0.113 at 0.5 alpha level with 348 degrees of freedom. The R-Square value of 0.96 predicts 96 percent of the relationship between accountability of the leaders in Lutheran Church of Nigeria and members' perception of their leadership effectiveness.

It was also deemed necessary to find out the extent of the variance of each case of the independent variable (accountability of the leaders in Lutheran Church of Nigeria and members' perception of their leadership effectiveness) as responded by each respondent (see Table 4).

Table 4. Analysis of Variance of the Relationship between Accountability of the Leaders in Lutheran Church of Nigeria and Members' Perception of Their Leadership Effectiveness

Model	Sum of Squares	Df	Mean Square	F	Sig.
Regression	826.65	1	826.65	3976.25	0.000b
Residual	71.93	346	0.21		
Total	898.59	347			

The above table presents the calculated F-value as (3976.25) and the P-value as (.000). Being that the P-value (.000) is below the probability level of 0.05, the result, therefore, means that there is a significant relationship between accountability of the leaders in Lutheran Church of Nigeria and members' perception of their leadership effectiveness

4.1.3 Hypothesis Three

The null hypothesis states that there is no significant relationship between the integrity of the leaders in Lutheran Church of Nigeria and their members' "followership." In order to test the hypothesis, regression analysis was performed on the data (see Table 5).

Table 5. Regression Analysis of the Relationship between the Integrity of the Leaders in Lutheran Church of Nigeria and Their Members' "Followership"

Model	R	R-Square	Adjusted R-Square	Std. the Error of the Estimate	R-Square Change
1	0.93*	0.87	0.87	0.49	0.87

*Significant at 0.05 level; df = 346; N = 348; critical R-value = 0.113

The table shows that the calculated R-value 0.93 was greater than the critical R-value of 0.113 at 0.5 alpha level with 348 degrees of freedom. The R-Square value of 0.87 predicts 87 percent of the relationship between the integrity of the leaders in Lutheran Church of Nigeria and their members' "followership."

It was also deemed necessary to find out the extent of the variance of each case of the independent variable (integrity of the leaders in Lutheran Church of Nigeria and their members' "followership") as indicated by each respondent (see Table 6).

Table 6. Analysis of Variance of the Relationship between the Integrity of the Leaders in Lutheran Church of Nigeria and Their Members' "Followership"

Model	Sum of Squares	Df	Mean Square	F	Sig.
Regression	564.43	1	564.43	2365.25	0.000b
Residual	82.57	346	0.24		
Total	647.00	347			

The above table presents the calculated F-value as (2365.25) and the P-value as (.000). Being that the P-value (.000) is below the probability level of 0.05, the result, therefore, means that there is a significant relationship between the integrity of the leaders in Lutheran Church of Nigeria and their members' "followership."

4.1.4 Hypothesis Four

The null hypothesis states that there is no significant relationship between accountability of the leaders in Lutheran Church of Nigeria and their members' "followership." In order to test the hypothesis, regression analysis was performed on the data (see Table 7).

Table 7. Regression Analysis of the Relationship between Accountability of the Leaders in Lutheran Church of Nigeria and Their Members' "Followership"

Model	R	R-Square	Adjusted R-Square	Std. the Error of the Estimate	R-Square Change
1	0.94*	0.88	0.88	0.47	0.88

*Significant at 0.05 level; df = 346; N = 348; critical R-value = 0.113

The table shows that the calculated R-value 0.94 was greater than the critical R-value of 0.113 at 0.5 alpha level with 346 degrees of freedom. The R-Square value of 0.94 predicts 94 percent of the relationship between accountability of the leaders in Lutheran Church of Nigeria and their members' "followership."

It was also deemed necessary to find out the extent of the variance of each case of the independent variable (accountability of the leaders in Lutheran Church of Nigeria and their members' "followership") as responded by each respondent (see Table 8).

Table 8. Analysis of Variance of the Relationship between Accountability of the Leaders in Lutheran Church of Nigeria and Their Members' "Followership"

Model	Sum of Squares	Df	Mean Square	F	Sig.
Regression	878.93	1	878.83	16393.19	0.000b
Residual	18.55	346	0.05		
Total	897.48	347			

The above table presents the calculated F-value as (16393.19) and the P-value as (.000). Being that the P-value (.000) is below the probability level of 0.05, the result, therefore, means that there is a significant relationship between accountability of the leaders in Lutheran Church of Nigeria and their members' "followership."

4.1.5 Hypothesis Five

The null hypothesis states that there is no significant influence of the integrity of the leaders in Lutheran Church of Nigeria and people's membership in the church. In order to test the hypothesis, regression analysis was performed on the data (see Table 9).

Table 9. Regression Analysis of the Influence of Integrity of the Leaders in Lutheran Church of Nigeria and People's Membership in the Church

Model	R	R-Square	Adjusted R-Square	Std. the Error of the Estimate	R-Square Change
1	0.99*	0.98	0.98	0.23	0.98

*Significant at 0.05 level; df= 346; N= 348; critical R-value = 0.113

The table shows that the calculated R-value 0.99 was greater than the critical R-value of 0.113 at 0.5 alpha level with 348 degrees of freedom. The R-Square value of 0.98 predicts 98 percent of the influence of integrity of the leaders in Lutheran Church of Nigeria and people's membership in the church.

It was also deemed necessary to find out the extent of the variance of each case of the independent variable (influence of integrity of the leaders in Lutheran Church of Nigeria and people's membership in the church) as responded by each respondent (see Table 10).

Table 10. Analysis of Variance of the Influence of Integrity of the Leaders in Lutheran Church of Nigeria and People's Membership in the Church

Model	Sum of Squares	Df	Mean Square	F	Sig.
Regression	878.93	1	878.93	16393.19	0.000b
Residual	18.55	346	0.05		
Total	897.48	347			

The above table presents the calculated F-value as (16393.19) and the P-value as (.000). Being that the P-value (.000) is below the probability level of 0.05, the result, therefore, means that there is a significant influence of integrity of the leaders in Lutheran Church of Nigeria and people's membership in the church.

4.1.6 Hypothesis Six

The null hypothesis states that there is no significant influence of accountability of the leaders in Lutheran Church of Nigeria and people's membership in the church. In order to test the hypothesis, regression analysis was performed on the data (see Table 11).

Table 11. Regression Analysis of the Influence of the Accountability of the Leaders in Lutheran Church of Nigeria and People's Membership in the Church

Model	R	R-Square	Adjusted R-Square	Std. the Error of the Estimate	R-Square Change
1	0.97*	0.93	0.93	0.42	0.93

*Significant at 0.05 level; df = 346; N = 348; critical R-value = 0.113

The table shows that the calculated R-value 0.97 was greater than the critical R-value of 0.113 at 0.5 alpha level with 346 degrees of freedom. The R-Square value of 0.93 predicts 93 percent of the influence of accountability of the leaders in Lutheran Church of Nigeria and people's membership in the church.

It was also deemed necessary to find out the extent of the variance of each case of the independent variable (influence of accountability of the leaders in Lutheran Church of Nigeria and people's membership in the church) as responded by each respondent (see Table 12).

Table 12. Analysis of Variance of the Influence of Accountability of the Leaders in Lutheran Church of Nigeria and People's Membership in the Church

Model	Sum of Squares	Df	Mean Square	F	Sig.
Regression	836.43	1	836.43	4740.36	0.000b
Residual	61.05	346	0.176		
Total	897.48	347			

The above table presents the calculated F-value as (4740.36) and the P-value as (.000). Being that the P-value (.000) is below the probability level of 0.05, the result, therefore, means that there is a significant influence of accountability of the leaders in Lutheran Church of Nigeria on people's membership in the church.

4.1.7 Hypothesis Seven

The null hypothesis states that there is no significant influence of age on the level of integrity of the leaders in Lutheran Church of Nigeria. In order to test the hypothesis, regression analysis was performed on the data (see Table 13).

Table 13. Regression Analysis of the Influence of Age on the Level of Integrity of the Leaders in Lutheran Church of Nigeria

Model	R	R-Square	Adjusted R-Square	Std. the Error of the Estimate	R-Square Change
1	0.97*	0.93	0.93	0.42	0.93

*Significant at 0.05 level; df = 346; N = 348; critical R-value = 0.113

The table shows that the calculated R-value 0.97 was greater than the critical R-value of 0.113 at 0.5 alpha level with 346 degrees of freedom. The R-Square value of 0.97 predicts 97 percent of the influence of age on the level of integrity of the leaders in Lutheran Church of Nigeria.

It was also deemed necessary to find out the extent of the variance of each case of the independent variable (influence of age on the level of integrity of the leaders in Lutheran Church of Nigeria) as responded by each respondent (see Table 14).

Table 14. Analysis of Variance of the Influence of Age on the Level of Integrity of the Leaders in Lutheran Church of Nigeria

Model	Sum of Squares	Df	Mean Square	F	Sig.
Regression	836.43	1	836.43	4740.36	0.000b
Residual	61.05	346	0.18		
Total	897.48	347			

The above table presents the calculated F-value as (4740.36) and the P-value as (.000). Being that the P-value (.000) is below the probability level of 0.05, the result, therefore, means that there is a significant influence of age on the level of integrity of the leaders in Lutheran Church of Nigeria.

4.1.8 Hypothesis Eight

The null hypothesis states that there is no significant influence of age on the accountability of the leaders in Lutheran Church of Nigeria. In order to test the hypothesis, two variables were identified as follows:

1. Age as an independent variable
2. Accountability of the leaders is the dependent variable

The independent t-test analysis was used in comparing the mean score of the two independent groups (see Table 15).

Table 15. Independent T-Test Analysis of the Influence of Age on the Accountability of the Leaders in Lutheran Church of Nigeria

Variable	N	X	SD	t
Older	255	12.41	1.08	
				20.36*
Younger	93	15.38	1.50	

*Significant at 0.05 level; df = 346; N= 348; critical t-value =1.960

As shown in Table 15, the calculated t-value is 20.36. This value was tested at 0.05 level with 346 degrees of freedom. The obtained t-value (20.36) is greater than the critical t-value (1.960). Hence the result was significant. The result, therefore, means that there is a significant influence of age on the accountability of the leaders in Lutheran Church of Nigeria.

4.1.9 Hypothesis Nine

The null hypothesis states that there is no significant difference in the level of integrity and accountability of the leaders in Lutheran Church of Nigeria identified with before and after the theological teaching.

The dependent t-test analysis was used in comparing the mean score of the two independent groups (see Table 16).

Table 16. Dependent T-Test Analysis of the Difference in the Level of Integrity and Accountability of the Leaders in Lutheran Church of Nigeria Identified with Before and After the Theological Teaching

Variable	N	X	SD	t
Integrity before teaching		13.32	1.68	
	348			331.69*
Integrity after teaching		16.33	1.68	
Accountability before teaching		10.22	1.78	
	348			238.57*
Accountability after teaching		13.20	1.78	

*Significant at 0.05 level; df = 346; N = 348; critical t-value =1.960

As shown in Table 16, integrity before and after the theological teaching of the leaders in Lutheran Church of Nigeria produced the calculated t-value of 331.69. This value was tested at 0.05 level with 346 degrees of freedom. The resulting t-value (331.69) was greater than the critical t-value (1.960). With respect to accountability, the calculated t-value was 238.57, when tested with the critical t-value at 0.05 with 346 degrees of freedom, was found greater than the critical t-value (1.960). Hence the results were significant. The result, therefore, means that there is a significant difference in the level of integrity and accountability of the leaders in Lutheran Church of Nigeria identified with before and after teaching, meaning that the level of integrity and accountability of the leaders in Lutheran Church of Nigeria was identified to be remarkably higher after theological teaching.

4.2 Discussion of Findings

The calculated R-value (0.98) was greater than the critical R-value (0.113) at 0.05 level with 346 degrees of freedom shows that the relationship between the integrity of the leaders in Lutheran Church of Nigeria and members' perception of their leadership effectiveness was significant. The result is in agreement with the research findings of Fry,[2] who found that where there is human leadership, there is the opportunity to exhibit a substantial level of integrity and accountability. The result of the findings also agreed with the findings of Awamleh and Gardner,[3] who observed that people can only lead those who build trust in them. In the basic sense, integrity and accountability mean to live out your life in private in the same way you live or talk about your life in public. The result of the analysis caused the null hypothesis to be rejected while the alternative one was retained.

The data analysis in Table 3 sought to find the relationship between accountability of the leaders in Lutheran Church of Nigeria and members' perception of their leadership effectiveness, It found a significant relationship between the two due to the fact that the calculated R-value (0.96) was greater than the critical R-value (0.113) at 0.05 level with 348 degrees of freedom. This result implies that there is a significant relationship between accountability of the leaders in Lutheran Church of Nigeria and members' perception of their leadership effectiveness. The result is in agreement with the research findings of Hartzog and others[4] who highlighted that leadership accountability is a condition in which people are required or expected to act consistently with their commitment and be responsible for their actions or decisions, including a response to circumstances. The result of the findings also agreed with the findings of Purvanova and others.[5] The result of the analysis caused the null hypothesis to be rejected while the alternative one was retained.

The data analysis in Table 5 sought to find the relationship between integrity of the leaders in Lutheran Church of Nigeria and their members' "followership." It determined that relationship was significant due to the fact that the calculated R-value (0.93) was greater than the critical R-value (0.113) at 0.05 level with 348 degrees of freedom. The result is in agreement with Hybels,[6] who concluded that leader are influencial not just because they are experienced but because their leadership styles are a perfect fit for the ministry needs of an organization. The result of the findings also agreed with the findings of Akpami,[7] who asserted that church leadership to some

---

[2] Fry, "Toward a Theory of Spiritual Leadership," 693.

[3] Awamleh and Gardner, "Perceptions of Leader Charisma and Effectiveness," 345.

[4] Hartog et al., "Culture Specific and Cross-Culturally Generalizable Implicit Leadership Theories," 219.

[5] Radostina K. Purvanova, Joyce E. Bono, and Jessica Dzieweczynski, "Transformational Leadership, Job Characteristics, and Organizational Citizenship Performance," *Human Performance* 19, no. 1 (January 2006): 1.

[6] Hybels, *Courageous Leadership*, 12.

[7] Akpami, *Vision: Equipping Church Workers for Effective Leadership*, 110.

extent is based on what is known as a divine calling.[8] The result of the analysis caused the null hypothesis to be rejected while the alternative one was retained.

The data analysis in Table 7 sought to find the relationship between accountability of the leaders in Lutheran Church of Nigeria and their members' "followership." It discovered a significant relationship due to the fact that the calculated R-value (0.94) was greater than the critical R-value (0.113) at 0.05 level with 346 degrees of freedom. The result is in agreement with the research findings of Okoronta,[9] who defined leadership as the ability to give guidance to those who will follow it to complete a mission statement in an organization like the church. The result of the findings also agreed with the findings of Nwolise,[10] who viewed leadership as a complex phenomenon which combines the personal traits of an individual and the dominant variables in an organization. The result of the analysis caused the null hypothesis to be rejected while the alternative one was retained.

The data analysis in Table 9 sought to find out the influence of integrity of the leaders in Lutheran Church of Nigeria on the membership of people in the church. The relationship was significant due to the fact that the calculated R-value (0.99) was greater than the critical R-value (0.113) at 0.05 level with 348 degrees of freedom. The result is in agreement with the research findings of Strudler and Warren,[11] who noted that leadership is a common phenomenon in every facet of life. The result of the findings also agreed with the findings of Munroe,[12] who asserted that leaders are those who accept or are placed in extraordinary circumstances which bring forth their latent physical and spiritual potentials, such as producing a character that implies confidence and trust of their followers or members of God. The result of the analysis caused the null hypothesis to be rejected while the alternative one was retained.

The data analysis in Table 11 sought to find out the influence of accountability of the leaders in Lutheran Church of Nigeria and membership of people in the church. It was significant due to the fact that the calculated R-value (0.97) was greater than the critical R-value (0.113) at 0.05 level with 346 degrees of freedom. The result is in agreement with the definition of

---

[8] Pastors are called by Christ into the office that He instituted.

[9] Okoronta, "The Impact of Leadership Styles in the Pentecostal Churches on the Growth of the Gospel in Kaduna State," 16.

[10] Nwolise, *Traditional Administration in Nigeria*, 12.

[11] Strudler and Warren, "Authority, Heuristics, and the Structure of Excuses," 159–78.

[12] Myles Munroe, *Becoming a Leader* (New Kensington, Penn.: Whitaker House, 2009).

Hornby,[13] who asserted that leadership is the ability to be a leader, showing the qualities of leadership is necessary for a team. The result of the findings also agreed with the findings of Ngu,[14] who sees the leader as a head whose vision is to depend heavily on the formal authority of the office to ensure obedience from members of the organization. But note well, obedience to the pastor is only in so far as the pastor remains faithful to God's Word in both his teaching and in his life. The result of the analysis caused the null hypothesis to be rejected while the alternative one was retained.

The data analysis in Table 13 sought to find out the influence of age on the level of integrity of the leaders in Lutheran Church of Nigeria. This relationship was significant due to the fact that the calculated R-value (0.97) was greater than the critical R-value (0.113) at 0.05 level with 346 degrees of freedom. The result is in agreement with the research findings of Laub,[15] who noted that the stronger an organization scores in servant leadership practices when compared to paternalistic or autocratic leadership practices, the healthier the organization. The result of the survey also agreed with the findings of Albritton, Oswald, and Anderson,[16] who observed that leaders often are pressured by corporate executives functioning in maintaining ethical values while working to increase the profitability of their corporations, such as principled risk-takers and conventional decision-makers. The result of the analysis caused the null hypothesis to be rejected while the alternative one was retained.

The data analysis in Table 15 sought to find out the influence of age on the accountability of the leaders in Lutheran Church of Nigeria, The results were significant due to the fact that the calculated t-value (20.36) was greater than the critical t-value (1.960) at 0.05 level with 346 degrees of freedom. The result is in agreement with the research findings of Okoronta,[17] who observes that leadership in church specifically involves a series of vital roles, such as teaching, counseling, discipline, policy implementation, and coordination, recruitment of staff, and retirement of staff for the growth of the organization. The result of the survey also agreed with the findings of Becker,[18] who noticed that it is only church leaders with high integrity who can make excellent candidates for leadership positions because they will not

[13] Albert Sydney Hornby, *Oxford Advanced Learner's Dictionary of Current English* (Oxford: Oxford University Press, 2001), 19.

[14] Ngu, *Management Principles and Workers Motivation in Nigeria*, 12.

[15] Laub, "Organizational Health," 112.

[16] Albritton, Oswald, and Anderson, "Leadership Quality and Follower Affect," 10.

[17] Okoronta, "The Impact of Leadership Styles in the Pentecostal Churches on the Growth of the Gospel in Kaduna State," 16.

[18] Becker, "Integrity in Organizations," 160.

steal organizations' resources, treat others unfairly, or deceive themselves or others. The result of the analysis caused the null hypothesis to be rejected while the alternative one was retained.

The data analysis in Table 16 sought to find out the difference in the level of integrity and accountability of the leaders in Lutheran Church of Nigeria before and after theological teaching. The relationship was significant due to the fact that the calculated t-value for integrity before and after teaching (331.67) was greater than the critical t-value (1.960) at 0.05 level with 346 degrees of freedom. Regarding accountability before and after teaching, the calculated T-value (331.69) was greater than the critical T-value (1.960) at 0.05 level with 346 degrees of freedom. This result implies that there is a significant difference in the level of integrity and accountability of the leaders in Lutheran Church of Nigeria identified with before and after teaching. The result is in agreement with Mills,[19] who maintained that the church provides regular opportunities for members to express their points of view and opinions, and to seek their input on proposed plans. The result also agrees with the findings of Berger,[20] who asserted that the functioning of a church is not that different from other groups or organizations; there are many similarities. The result of the analysis caused the null hypothesis to be rejected while the alternative one was retained.

[19] Heward-Mills, *The Art of Leadership*, 11.

[20] Berger, *The Desecularization of the World*, 131.

CHAPTER FIVE

SUMMARY, CONCLUSIONS, AND RECOMMENDATIONS

5.1 Summary of the Study

This study was conducted in order to look for a way of strengthening integrity and accountability in the leadership of Lutheran Church of Nigeria. In order to carry out the study, seven specific objectives were drawn from which nine null hypotheses and six research questions were formulated.

The specific objectives are as follows:

1. To examine the level of integrity and accountability in the leadership of Lutheran Church of Nigeria.
2. To find out different elements of dishonesty and nonaccountability found in some leaders in Lutheran Church of Nigeria.
3. To find out the possible factors which bring about dishonesty and nonaccountability among leaders of Lutheran Church of Nigeria.
4. To determine the intent behind and reasons to strengthen integrity and accountability in the leadership of Lutheran Church of Nigeria.
5. To find out the barriers to the effective strengthening of integrity and accountability in the leadership of Lutheran Church of Nigeria.
6. To determine the strategies that can help strengthen the integrity and accountability of church leaders in Nigeria.
7. To make useful recommendations on how to strengthen the teaching of theology in Lutheran Church of Nigeria and beyond.

The related literature was reviewed based on the variables in the above specific objectives. The review was done to examine research and expert opinions on leadership, principally of journals and textbooks. A survey was designed that allowed for the use of a questionnaire entitled "Integrity and Accountability Strengthening in Church Leadership Questionnaire (IASCLQ)." A sample size of 348 was used for the study

Respondents were selected through the use of the proportional stratified random sampling technique. Data collected were subjected to statistical analysis and interpretation. From the result of the data analysis, it was observed that there is a significant relationship between the integrity of the leaders in Lutheran Church of Nigeria and members' perception of their leadership effectiveness. A leader leads those who can build trust in him. This is achievable through the leader walking in the path of Christ and steering clear of hypocrisy. It is a call to the highest of ideals, "death to self," and "the last shall be the first." A leader should steer clear from dishonesty, duplicity, corruption, discontentment, and hypocrisy.

When evil traits are seen in the life of a church leader, Christ's good name is defamed, and He is defiled with feeble words and/or excuses. Integrity is therefore considered the highest application of virtues. It is the demonstration of who the church leader is in Christ Jesus and a demonstration that his faith is real and backed up with his attitude and words.

Luther, in answer to the question "How God's name is kept holy," says:

> God's name is kept holy when the Word of God is taught in its truth and purity, and we, as the children of God, also lead holy lives according to it. Help us to do this, dear Father in heaven! But anyone who teaches or lives contrary to God's Word profanes the name of God among us. Protect us from this, heavenly Father![1]

It is essential to pursue integrity in the leadership of the Lutheran Church of Nigeria and ensure that the transformational work of Christ is real and manifest. Thus Paul explains what it means to live in complete submission to Christ: use spiritual gifts to serve others and genuinely love others (Romans 12).

There is a significant relationship between accountability in Lutheran Church of Nigeria and members' perception of their leadership effectiveness, and there is significant relationship between the integrity of the leaders in Lutheran Church of Nigeria and their members' "followership."

Accountability in church leadership means transparency and reporting. Reporting is explaining what we are doing so that we can be held responsible and answerable for our decisions and actions. Reporting is explaining how we responded to various situations. These decisions, actions, and responses should be consistent with our commitment to God and to other Christians.

> According to the grace of God given to me, like a skilled master builder I laid a foundation, and someone else is building upon it. Let each one

[1] Luther, *Luther's Small Catechism with Explanation*, 20.

> take care how he builds upon it. For no one can lay a foundation other than that which is laid, which is Jesus Christ. Now if anyone builds on the foundation with gold, silver, precious stones, wood, hay, straw—each one's work will become manifest, for the Day will disclose it, because it will be revealed by fire, and the fire will test what sort of work each one has done. If the work that anyone has built on the foundation survives, he will receive a reward. If anyone's work is burned up, he will suffer loss, though he himself will be saved, but only as through fire. (1 Cor. 3:10–15)

It is a precept of demonstrating transparency so that we seek help in areas of our weakness and struggle, and understanding where and how we are growing for encouragement. This, in effect, helps the leadership stay on track and get proper care and support. Jesus said, "Everyone to whom much was given, of him much will be required, and from him to whom they entrusted much, they will demand the more" (Luke 12:48).

Leadership styles should reflect the gifts of individual leaders. But above all, the character of integrity should be exhibited in the obedience and practice of the moral care of the ethics, morals, value, and precepts of God's Word. In practice, integrity will produce honor, truth, and reliability. This will lead to deeper relations and, of course, development and confidence and the Christian faith.

When Jesus calls us to integrity, He means that we should be true to our word as a testimony to our faith in Him. Our "yes" should be "yes" and our "no" should be "no." Church leaders who use God's name in order to perform or claim to perform supernatural things with the help of the devil are not exhibiting integrity. Fortune-telling, casting spells, and other occult practices such as those dominating the African Independent Churches do not represent Christ who is living in us!

> There shall not be found among you anyone who burns his son or his daughter as an offering, anyone who practices divination or tells fortunes or interprets omens, or a sorcerer, or a charmer, or a medium or a necromancer or one who inquires of the dead, for whoever does these things is an abomination to the LORD. And because of these abominations the LORD your God is driving them out before you. (Deut. 18:10–12)

Every leader's "help is in the name of the LORD, who made heaven and earth" (Ps. 124:8).

The report also observes that there is a significant relationship between accountability of the leaders in Lutheran Church of Nigeria and their members' "followership." Holding leaders accountable for their teaching and life helps leaders maintain the highest standards of ethical and moral behavior.

There is a significant influence on the integrity of the leaders in Lutheran Church of Nigeria and people's membership in the church. Members of the church can only perceive their leaders' performance effectiveness if the leadership is honest to the people they are leading.

Every leader has intentions; the intention may be positive or negative, good or bad, beneficial to either the leader or to the members. However, a successful Christian ministry is founded, first and foremost, on a common commitment of both leaders and members to be and remain faithful to God's Word. On that basis, shared goals and objectives are established and the leader and members work together. This will lead to the growth of the church and its increase in "followership"/membership strength.

There is a significant difference in the level of integrity and accountability of the leaders in Lutheran Church of Nigeria identified with before and after teaching. Theological teaching is the basis for strengthening integrity and accountability in church leadership. Christ justifies every Christian leader for service in good works. Every Christian church leader dies through real unity with the body of the crucified Christ. This is the truth! We should praise God for truth and then work in the light of the truth, having ascertained that the Lord blesses obedience, but our obedience is to be out of love for Christ, not out of constraint and our desire to puff up ourselves.

In John 15, those who abide in the vine (Christ Jesus) will bring forth much fruit (good works). The result of being released from the Law and joined to Christ involves a change in allegiance. Godly fruits exist in transformed lives that manifest godly attitudes and actions. The fruits of the Holy Spirit in a believer's life are manifested internally in attitudes of "love, joy, peace, patience, kindness, goodness, faithfulness, gentleness, and self-control" (Gal. 5:22).

In Hebrews, the writer speaks of the "fruit of lips that acknowledge His name" (Heb. 13:15), and apostle Paul's prayer that the Philippian believers would be prepared for the day of Christ by being "filled with the fruit of righteousness that comes through Jesus Christ, to the glory and praise of God" (Phil. 1:11).

Christian church leaders have been released from the Law (Rom. 7:6). By virtue of our death with Christ on the cross through Baptism, we have been freed from the Law just as women in the New Testament times were freed from the laws that bound them to their deceased husbands (Rom. 7:2–3). St. Paul uses marriage to illustrate our relationship to the Law and declares that salvation can be found only in Jesus (cf. Acts 4:12; Rom. 7:1–4). The result: Christian leaders are no longer under the Law. The spirit of freedom does not give us the right to do whatever we want; rather, it is the gift of a new life in Christ by which we are given the desire and the gift of the Holy Spirit to do what is pleasing in His sight. Life as a Christian leader is not as has unfortunately been portrayed by some. It is simply working out what God in Jesus Christ worked in us (cf. Phil. 2:12)!

So serving in the newness of the Spirit should cause us to ponder:

1. Is this not a fulfillment of Ezekiel's prophecy of the new covenant where God promised a spiritual "heart transplant" for Israel (Ezek. 36:26), first fulfilled by Jesus with the Jewish disciples in His last Passover (Luke 22:15) and later fulfilled by the church at Corinth composed of Gentiles and Jews (1 Cor. 11:25) to proclaim the Lord's death until He comes?
2. A new heart gives new ability to obey.
3. Man's responsibility is to do good works (walk in God's statutes and keep His ordinances).
4. God's sovereign gift of grace is the gift of the heart of flesh—a heart to obey out of love and a desire to be pleasing to the Father.

Christian church leaders are led by the Holy Spirit; therefore, they must be spiritual. They continue serving Christ not in the human nature, but without fear, in holiness and righteousness, with sincerity and joy. We can say with the psalmist: "Oh how I love Your law" (Ps. 119:97). God's Law in our heart is rather the law of love. And we obey that law because we fear and love the Lord.

Integrity and accountability in the leadership of Lutheran Church of Nigeria is strengthened through the teaching of the theological truth that leaders are being united by Christ in life so that, walking with our Lord and Savior, they can go from "no" power of the flesh to "all" power in Christ who strengthens us (Phil. 4:13).

5.2 Conclusions

Based on the findings of the research work, these conclusions follow:

1. There is significant relationship between integrity of the leaders in Lutheran Church of Nigeria and members' perception of their leadership effectiveness.
2. There is significant relationship between accountability of the leaders in Lutheran Church of Nigeria and members' perception of their leadership effectiveness.
3. There is significant relationship between integrity of the leaders in Lutheran Church of Nigeria and their members' "followership."

4. There is significant relationship between accountability of the leaders in Lutheran Church of Nigeria and their members' "followership."
5. There is significant influence of integrity of the leaders in Lutheran Church of Nigeria and people's membership in the church.
6. There is significant influence of accountability of the leaders in Lutheran Church of Nigeria and people's membership in the church.
7. There is significant influence of age on the level of integrity of the leaders in Lutheran Church of Nigeria.
8. There is significant influence of age on the accountability of the leaders in Lutheran Church of Nigeria.
9. There is significant difference in the level of integrity and accountability of the leaders in Lutheran Church of Nigeria identified before and after teaching.

The above conclusion explains that the null hypotheses in 1.5 have changed in the course of experiment. In null hypotheses, Ho always uses the equals sign, which means everything remains the same. In alternative hypotheses, Ho always uses the sign of inequality, which means that everything has changed. The changes from the hypotheses are as a result of the series of theological teachings which were carried out. Thus there is a significant relationship between the different variables of the experiments.

5.3 Recommendations

It is recommended that in order to achieve integrity and accountability in church leadership:

1. Church leaders should be good examples for the members by way of presenting themselves with a high level of integrity and accountability as well as making themselves excellent candidates for leadership positions. Tables 4–6 present the result that there is increase in "followership" of leadership with high levels of integrity and accountability.
2. Leaders should be active and bold to uphold justice and maintain honesty in the church.
3. Leaders should be serious in their quest to show effective service to God, knowing well that the followers are bound to be influenced by their actions. Experiment Tables 12 and 13 are regression analyses of the influence of leadership effectiveness.

4. Church management should ensure that there is regular training for pastors and other leaders with great expectation that the training will build positive impact on their service to God who called them. Tables 15 and 16 confirm that teachings increased both the integrity and accountability of leaders.
5. Leaders must be faithful, trustworthy, kind, and most important, God-fearing to be able to control the affairs of the church as well as the members.
6. Committees need to be set and responsibilities delegated to others to be part of the church leadership. The best-practice model of accountability is here emphasized.
7. Leadership in churches goes along with high level of responsibility, and in order to achieve its primary objective, which is the growth of the Gospel proclamation, accountability is required. Members' "followership" and cooperation seem to be on the increase when church leaders exhibit the character as well as a personality that bring good personal interactions and relationships between them. Good interpersonal interactions and relationships tend to promote leader's integrity before their followers, coupled with making their followers in church respect the leadership.

This study offered me an opportunity for collegial discussion of theological issues in all the courses, which helped deepen my theological person through a trajectory of growth. This project will have a great impact on Lutheran Church of Nigeria and perhaps a great impact on Lutheran church bodies in Africa and beyond.

Recent grants to Lutheran Church of Nigeria from the Lutheran Women's Missionary League (LWML) for Nigeria Seminary Dormitory Renovation, the Mission Advancement Funds for Recovery of Nigeria Seminary Library, and the International Guests Quarters Renovation promise a new dawn in the church. The leadership of the church resolved to build from scratch and to finish a brand-new dormitory facility instead of the renovation of old dormitories with weak foundations and frames using the same amount of grant. The new dormitory and quarters accommodate more students and guests respectively with modern facilities. They assist in fulfilling the standard of the Nigerian University Commission. The seminary library building work is aggressively progressing. It never used to be like that in the past. Integrity and accountability were not considered important in the leadership of the church.

The impact of this project "Strengthening Integrity and Accountability in the Leadership of Lutheran Church of Nigeria" will not be limited to

Lutheran Church of Nigeria but will go a long way to help other African Lutheran churches in the International Lutheran Council (ILC), particularly as I have served as the chairman of the Africa region.

It is worthy of note that the growth of integrity and accountability in the leadership of Lutheran Church of Nigeria will be monitored through continued teachings and evaluation of actual performances of leaders. The use of knowledge derived from this project to teach integrity, accountability, honesty, and good leadership to church leaders and members will affect our immediate society. This work is relevant to the everyday experience of human life in a fallen world, and it provides a correct biblical and theological perspective concerning the issues of dishonesty and nonaccountability of church leaders not only in Lutheran Church of Nigeria but also in the Christian churches as well.

This project is also important to Nigerian society because it will help to quell the heightened tension created by the high level of dishonesty, discontentment, nonaccountability, and lack of integrity of the leaders in our churches. The study is also significant as accountability, honesty, and a high degree of integrity of the church leaders are demanded as an example to leaders in government and other social, economic, and political organizations in Nigeria.

APPENDIX ONE

Letter of Introduction

Concordia Theological Seminary
6600 N. Clinton Street
Fort Wayne IN 46825

Dear Respondent,

I am a Doctor of Ministry (D.Min) student of Concordia Theological Seminary, Ft. Wayne, Indiana, the USA, conducting a study to find out a way(s) of strengthening integrity and accountability in the Leadership of the Lutheran Church of Nigeria. I am requesting you to kindly respond to the most appropriate option of this questionnaire as the information supplied by you will be treated with high level of confidentiality and used for academic purpose only. Your prompt response will be of great help to me. I appreciate your understanding and cooperation.

Thank you.

Yours faithfully,
CHRISTIAN EKONG
(*Researcher*)

APPENDIX TWO

Integrity and Accountability Strengthening in Church Leadership Questionnaire (IASCLQ)

Section A: (Personal Data)

(Please tick (√) the most appropriate box)

1. Location of home:
   - (a) Rural area ( )
   - (b) Urban area ( )
2. Position:
   - (a) LCN Board of Directors ( )
   - (b) Members of LCN Zonal Boards ( )
   - (c) Members of LCN District Boards ( )
   - (d) LCN Church Councilors ( )
   - (e) LCN Seminary Faculty Members ( )
   - (f) LCN Schools Management Board Members ( )
   - (g) Lutheran High Schools Principals ( )
   - (h) Past Presidents of LCN ( )
   - (i) Past Vice Presidents of LCN ( )
   - (j) Past District Chairmen-Lay ( )
   - (k) other workers of the church ( )
3. Age:
   - (a) Less than 21 years ( )
   - (b) 21–30 years ( )
   - (c) 31–40 years ( )
   - (d) 41 years and above ( )

4. Marital status:
   (a) Single ( )
   (b) Married ( )
   (c) Divorced ( )
   (d) Separated ( )
   (e) Widowed ( )
5. Your highest educational qualifications:
   (a) FSLC ( )
   (b) School Certificate ( )
   (c) Tertiary Institution Certificate ( )

SECTION B: (MAIN VARIABLES).

Instruction: Please tick (√) the most appropriate boxes

SA = Strongly Agree

A = Agree

D = Disagree

SD = Strongly Disagree

S/N	ITEMS	SA	A	D	SD
	ACCOUNTABILITY				
1.	Offering in every service are recorded				
2.	Tithe booklets are controlled by the treasurers				
3.	Income and expenses records are open to members of the church				
4.	The church has a joint account				
5.	The church has a good team of the Financial Committee that strictly controls disbursement of the money				
	DISHONESTY				
6.	Our pastors are not truthful				
7.	There is no trust among leaders				
8.	Pastors give false information sometimes				
9.	Some of the pastors are unreliable leaders				
10.	Some of our pastors are identified with deception				

	FOLLOWERSHIP				
11.	Members believe in their pastors				
12.	Pastors are regarded as role models				
13.	Members respond to church directives willingly				
14.	Members are proud of their leaders				
15.	Members follow the teaching of pastors				
	INTEGRITY				
16.	The pastors and leaders are highly respected				
17.	Leaders keep their words				
18.	The pastors are seen as the men of truth				
19.	The leaders are upright				
20.	The leaders and pastors have a good reputation outside				
	NONACCOUNTABILITY				
21.	There is no proper record keeping				
22.	Church budgets are open to members				
23.	Seeds, tithe, and offerings are not recorded				
24.	There is no account rendering after any project done				
25.	The church money is run by the pastor alone				
	FACTORS THAT BRING ABOUT DISHONESTY AND NONINTEGRITY				
26.	Poverty on the part of the pastors				
27.	Hardship in the land				
28.	The inborn trait of the pastor				
29.	Pastors exposure to a big sum of money				
30.	Lack of contentment on the part of the pastors				
	PURPOSE OF INTEGRITY AND ACCOUNTABILITY				
31.	Pastors encouragement to the members in faith				
32.	Members respect their leaders				
33.	Steady church growth				
34.	Emulation by the members				
35.	Leadership by example				

	BARRIERS TO EFFECTIVE STRENGTHENING OF INTEGRITY AND ACCOUNTABILITY				
36.	Leaders unaccountability to anyone				
37.	Pastors' luxurious lifestyles				
38.	The pastor's inherent dishonesty				
39.	Leaders use the church properties as a reward for their labor				
40.	The pastor's pomposity				
	STRATEGY THAT CAN HELP STRENGTHEN INTEGRITY AND ACCOUNTABILITY				
41.	Discipline to lack of integrity				
42.	Regular seminar to the church leaders				
43.	Division of labor				
44.	Appointment of leaders by merit				
45.	Proper care to the pastors				
	MEMBERS' PERCEPTION OF LEADERS' EFFECTIVENESS				
46.	Leaders visit their members				
47.	The leaders are members confident				
48.	The leaders are role models				
49.	Members' ideas are needed				
50.	The leaders are respected				
	MEMBERS' FOLLOWERSHIP				
51.	In our church, there is an increase in membership strength				
52.	There is an effective evangelism				
53.	Members are improved				
54.	Members massively go out to invite people to church				
55.	In our church, church planting is carried out regularly				

APPENDIX THREE

Council Paper Presentation Strengthening Integrity and Accountability in the Leadership of the Lutheran Church of Nigeria[1]

By Christian Okon Ekong President/Archbishop

1. Introduction

In today's world, people with accountability and integrity are hard to come by. It is quite disheartening that some church leaders no longer show integrity and accountability. Church leaders fail in their responsibilities to others in the church because most of them are not conscious of the fact that they can be tempted to misuse authority. The shepherding of the church is in the hands of the bishops, pastors, teachers, evangelists, elders, etc. Yet this is not an excuse to abuse the influence granted to them by exploiting people, misdirecting and misapplying the resources at their disposal. Promotion from one position to another in the church is not to make leaders forgetful of the fact that they are called to represent Christ, the Chief Shepherd and Bridegroom of the Church, as stewards.

Some leaders are fine Christians until they are selected to positions of leadership. Once the position is gained, they start teaching the people demeaning, derogatory ways and sometimes make excessive demands on the people, as well as showing some levels of dishonesty and nonaccountability. Also, church leaders fail in their bids to discharge their responsibilities acceptably. Besides ignorance, they can be tempted to abuse their authority. The truth is that the roles of bishops, pastors, evangelists, and other church leaders are not to hold down the people and have them serve their needs and wants but rather that they (leaders) equip and elevate those they lead to serve Jesus and change the world—the example of Jesus' leadership, who came to serve and not to be served, is here emphasized.

---

[1] Lecture Presentation at LCN 38th Council. Aspects of this presentation have been modified for publication in this book.

When church leaders understand that the authority God has given them is not for themselves, but for all sorts and conditions of people placed under them, then the virtue of integrity and accountability will be strengthened. Furthermore, church leaders are exposed to the temptation of profiting in their privileges. When church leaders decide to profit from the privilege of leadership, it gives the people the reason to question their motives. That notwithstanding, pastors can be appreciated by the members of the church with gifts they give out of godly generosity. Regular devotionals exercises like prayerful reading of Holy Scripture will help to curb and reduce the present lack of integrity and will aid in holding leaders accountable. Leaders are to exercise their authority in a faithful manner, keeping with the standards of God's Word, not merely "wielding authority." Peterson summarizes this in *Working the Angles* as faith responding willingly to Christ's commands.[2]

This presentation is therefore intended to fill an existing gap by addressing teachings for strengthening integrity and accountability in the leadership of the Lutheran Church.

2. Identification of Context

Two of the fundamental traits of quality church leadership are integrity and accountability. Lack of these elements brings about discouragement among members and people generally. Consider this most famous New Testament command for Christian living:

> But the fruit of the Spirit is love, joy, peace, patience, kindness, goodness, faithfulness, gentleness, and self-control; against such things there is no law. And those who belong to Christ Jesus have crucified the flesh with its passion and desires. If we live by the Spirit, let us also keep in step with the Spirit. (Gal. 5:22–25)

This is a command to live a life of the highest integrity and accountability. In short, the expectation that church leaders demonstrate integrity and accountability. The Scriptures call for us to turn away from evil and do good. How much more is this true for Church leaders? 1 Peter says:

> Whoever desires to love life and see good days, . . . let him turn away from evil and do good; let him seek peace and pursue it. For the eyes of the Lord are upon the righteous, and His ears are open to their prayer. But the face of the Lord is against those who do evil. (3:10–12)

This definition of integrity calls a church leader to walk in the path of Christ and to steer clear of hypocrisy. There are even greater expectations for church leaders and teachers than for Christians. As James 3:1 says, "Not many of you should become teachers, my brothers, for you know that we

[2] Peterson, *Working the Angles*, 167.

who teach will be judged with greater strictness." The antonyms of integrity include dishonesty, duplicity, corruption, and hypocrisy. When evil traits are carried out by church leaders, Christ's good name is misrepresented, and He is defiled with feeble words and/or excuses. Integrity is one of the most important goals for a church leader because it demonstrates a connection between words and deed; it helps demonstrate that church leaders are servants of Christ Jesus. The absence of integrity in a church leader may indicate that he is self-serving or a fraud. Integrity needs to be pursued in the leadership of the Lutheran Church of Nigeria so that the transforming work of Christ can be seen by the people. Thus Paul explains what it means to live in complete submission to Christ: use spiritual gifts to serve others and genuinely love others (Romans 12).

2.1 Accountability

The church leader and people hold each other in mutual accountability. An accountable leader operates with checks on his actions. The people also are checked against being unfair toward the leader. The church leader is checked to make sure what he says he is doing is what in fact he is doing. This also gives the people confidence that their leader has their best interests in mind and is being a good steward of the gifts God has provided. Each leader builds off the work of previous leaders, and future leaders will build off his work. Ultimately, the Lord will reveal whether someone's work was straw or gold.

> According to the grace of God given to me, like a skilled master builder I laid a foundation, and someone else is building upon it. Let each one take care how he builds upon it. For no one can lay a foundation other than that which is laid, which is Jesus Christ. Now if anyone builds on the foundation with gold, silver, precious stones, wood, hay, straw—each one's work will become manifest, for the Day will disclose it, because it will be revealed by fire, and the fire will test what sort of work each one has done. If the work that anyone has built on the foundation survives, he will receive a reward. If anyone's work is burned up, he will suffer loss, though he himself will be saved, but only as through fire. (1 Cor. 3:10–15)

This liability, responsibility, and answerability on the part of church leaders focuses on sharing, in confidence and in trust, our heartfelt Christian sojourn. Then we can answer for our actions and know in which areas we struggle and need encouragement and growth. The precepts help us to stay on track and get proper care and support when we fail. We can be guideposts for one another in order to keep going. The reality of the Scripture is that every person—Christian and non-Christian—is accountable before the sovereign God and will one day have to bow before Christ. Jesus said, "Everyone to whom much was given, of him much will be required, and from him to whom they entrusted much, they will demand the more" (Luke 12:48). The reality of accountability cannot be rejected in church leadership.

3. Self-Description

Church leaders throughout the ages have struggled to remain faithful and able to serve throughout their lifetimes. Church leaders can fail for biblical reasons that disqualify them from continuing in their positions. Church leaders also end up dying in office, sometimes killed by opponents or others who disliked their leadership—this has happened in Africa not just a few times. Other causes have affected the time of a leader, such as burnout and depression. While the psychological and emotional struggles of burnout and depression seem to affect more church leaders in the West, graft and corruption as well as a lack of integrity seem to affect more leaders in Africa. Each age, place, and culture has its own temptations that affect church leaders where they serve. The goal of every church leader should be that of St. Paul, "I have fought the good fight; I have finished the race; I have kept the faith" (2 Tim. 4:7)

An article by Dean Carlson, "What Are the Behaviors That Will Destroy Leaders?"[3] looks at this problem from an African perspective. Carlson notes that the African church leader will encounter many pitfalls that will either discourage them, cause their work to stagnate, or worst yet bring shame and disrepute to the Gospel. He cites Dr. J. Robert Clinton, a professor at Fuller Theological Seminary, who studied a number of leaders in the Old and New Testament. He came to the startling conclusion that only 30 percent of the leaders mentioned in the Old and New Testaments finished well. He identified six items that caused leaders to either fail or not perform as well: (1) The Misuse of Money, (2) The Abuse of Power, (3) Pride, (4) Sexual Misconduct, (5) Family Troubles, and (6) Complacency. The article goes on to give specific examples of these items from various churches in Africa. No doubt, we have witnessed all these things in Nigeria too. The article continues with factors that contributed to successful leadership.

3.1 Lifelong Perspective and Learning Attitude

Effective leaders engage in lifelong learning. Learning does not stop when school ends. Top business leaders and executives frequently talk about the books they read throughout the year. Brian Evans of *Inc. Magazine* reported that most CEOs read a book a week.[4] Former CEO of Microsoft,

[3] Dean Carlson, "What Are the Behaviors That Will Destroy Leaders?" *Church Leader in Africa*, 1998. https://likeateam.com/what-are-the-behaviors-that-will-destroy-leaders/.

[4] Brian D. Evans, "Most CEOs Read A Book A Week. This Is How You Can Too (According To This Renowned Brain Coach)," *Inc.*, Published June 27, 2017, https://www.inc.com

Bill Gates releases his personal book reading list each year.[5] These CEOs of top companies recognize two main things: (1) they need a break from the day-to-day grind of work and (2) they need to get fresh ideas, sometimes from fields unrelated to their work, to stay sharp. Continued learning is very important for the church leader as is taking time to re-energize. As the CEOs of companies show, re-energizing is not going away for days or weeks at a time (though that may be appropriate once a year or so) but taking a few hours each week to engage in things not directly related to one's primary job. This is all the more important for the church leader who not only needs to balance physical and mental fitness but also spiritual fitness by staying nourished by the Word of God.

Effective leaders realize learning never ends. They continue to grow and seek improvement their entire lives. The author of Hebrews writes: Remember your leaders, those who spoke to you the word of God. Consider the outcome of their way of life, and imitate their faith. Jesus Christ is the same yesterday and today and forever (Hebrews 13:7–8).

3.2 Spiritual Renewal and Discipline

Closely connected with lifelong learning is spiritual renewal. It is essential for the church leader to continue the study of the Word of God As many pastors have found through the years, the preparations of Bible studies and sermons do not necessarily help a person stay fresh and engaged. It can be helpful to withdraw from the everyday work situation to remove the cares and needs of the job. In a place away from the day-to-day activities, study the Word of God, engage in prayer and contemplation. Jesus Himself took the disciples away from the crowd so they could rest and have renewal. This is helpful for a leader who intends to serve for a long time.

After he had been in ministry for about twenty-one years, Paul wrote: "I discipline my body and keep it under control, lest after preaching to others I myself should be disqualified" (1 Cor. 9:27). Some fifteen years later, when he was probably between sixty-five and seventy years old, Paul shared time-tested advice with Pastor Timothy: "Train yourself for godliness; for bodily training is of some value, godliness is of value in every way, as it holds promise for the present life and also for the life to come" (1 Tim. 4:7–8). Lifelong spiritual training made it possible for Paul to finish strongly.

/brian-d-evans/most-ceos-read-a-book-a-week-this-is-how-you-can-too-according-to-this-renowned-.html

[5] Bill Gates, "Looking for a summer read? Try one of these 5 books," *Gates Notes*, published May 20, 2019, https://www.gatesnotes.com/About-Bill-Gates/Summer-Books-2019.

3.3 Mentoring

The issue of mentoring is critically important in Africa. A top Zimbabwean church planter reflected that the first thing a church leader needed to do was to surround himself with godly men. The leader should give these godly men permission to counsel and rebuke him. These godly men serve as mentors and help hold the leader accountable. The godly men pray for the leader and offer a sounding board with whom the leader can share successes, failures, and problems. This sort of counsel has served to build the success of good leaders.

Dr. Richard Clinton's research has revealed that most leaders who have finished well have had 10 to 15 significant people who came alongside to help them at various stages in life. Clinton advises that if a leader wants to finish well, the leader needs to find mentors who hold him accountable in every aspect of his life. These mentors will help a leader avoid pitfalls and help a leader grow and develop to be his best.[6] This is what we need to consider very important as emerging leaders at various levels in the Lutheran Church of Nigeria.

We are engaged in this presentation to contribute toward the improvement of accountability and integrity in the leadership of the Lutheran Church of Nigeria through teaching contentment. The use of knowledge derived from this presentation to teach integrity, accountability, honesty, and good leadership among church leaders and members will affect our immediate society. This presentation is relevant to the everyday experience of human life in a fallen world, and it works toward providing a correct biblical and theological perspective concerning the issues of dishonesty and nonaccountability of church leaders not only in Lutheran Church of Nigeria but also in other churches as well.[7]

This paper is also important to the Nigerian society because it will decrease the heightened tension created by the high level of dishonesty, nonaccountability, and lack of integrity of the leaders in our churches. It is also significant as accountability, honesty, and a high degree of integrity of the church leaders are demanding an example to leaders in government and other social, economic, and political organizations in Nigeria. This is brought by a theologically balanced view of honesty, integrity, and accountability of the leaders on the "followership" and membership of Christians in Nigeria.

---

[6] Van Gelder, *The Missional Church and Leadership Formation.*

[7] David B. Barrett et al., *World Christian Trends, AD 30–AD 2200: Interpreting the Annual Christian Megacensus* (Pasadena, Calif.: William Carey Library, 2001).

4. A Strong Theological Focus

This presentation will discuss the theological implications of teaching, counseling, discipline, policy implementation and coordination, and the need to change staff, for the good of the organization.[8] Often people follow a man who is disciplined; some follow a man who can teach and express fluently; and others follow a man who has the ability to coordinate, organize, and even recruit. "Followership" is a concept that has dimensions of application to the ministry of God.

Leadership accountability is a condition in which people are required or expected to act consistently with their commitment and be responsible for their actions or decisions, including a response to circumstances.[9] Leadership accountability describes a leader who owns all of his actions. All too often, people account for their unfulfilled promises by giving a circumstance-based explanation for why the result wasn't produced. Sometimes presenting a good story about why a result was not produced is often just as acceptable as actually producing the result. When leaders are able to lay out the actions they took and the actions they did not take that leads to an outcome.

Integrity is based upon the Ten Commandments. A lack of integrity is connected with breaking various commandments. Ultimately, a lack of integrity creates distrust in people. Integrity is earned as people watch a leader carry out his duties. A lack of integrity betrays trust. Integrity is important in church leadership because of its benefits to leaders: it protects church leaders (Ps. 25:21); it gives leaders confidence (Prov. 10: 9) to lead. Integrity enhances better decisions (Prov. 11:3); it reflects well on the Lord (1 Chron. 29:17); it sets leaders apart from others and creates trust in others. Integrity is taking in beatings.

Members of the church or any organization can only perceive their leaders' performance effectiveness if the leadership is honest with the people they are leading and possesses integrity. Hence the church leader who is not accountable to followers may have the disposition to dishonesty that would ridicule the integrity of the leader.

Every leadership has intentions; the intention may be positive or negative, good or bad, beneficial to either the leaders, the organization itself,

---

[8] Okoronta, "The Impact of Leadership Styles in the Pentecostal Churches on the Growth of the Gospel in Kaduna State."

[9] Dorothy O. Potter, "The Traits/Characteristics, Attitudes, and Effective Work Environments of Servant Leaders: A Delphi Study" (PhD, Capella University, 2009), accessed February 26, 2019, http://search.proquest.com/docview/305160274/abstract/344013EF0894095PQ/1.

or to the members of the organization.[10] A successful Christian ministry is founded first on the Gospel of Jesus Christ and on the core values that the people in a particular place have embraced to share and propagate the Gospel there. A skillful leader helps a diverse group of people who have different desires, priorities, and interests come and work together for these common goals. This will lead to the growth of the church and increase its "followership"/membership strength.

It is recommended that in order to achieve accountability and integrity in church, committees need to be set and responsibilities delegated to others to be part of the church leadership. Church leaders should develop a training program such as seminars and workshops to educate on the need for accountability. This will achieve accountability in every facet of church leadership and administration.

Leadership in churches goes along with high level of responsibility, and in order to achieve its primary objective, which is the growth of the Gospel proclamation, accountability is required. Members' "followership" and cooperation seem to be on the increase when the church leaders exhibit character as well as a personality that brings good interpersonal interactions between them. These good interpersonal interactions and relationships tend to promote leaders' integrity before their followers, coupled with making their followers in church respect the leadership.

5. CONCLUSION

This presentation will help endow us with theological knowledge on effective spiritual leadership with such components as accountability and integrity for church growth and development.[11] This would be applied toward strengthening integrity and accountability in the leadership of the Lutheran Church of Nigeria. Above all, this presentation calls on our congregations, districts, zonal superintendencies, schools, boards, and committees to identify the level of integrity and accountability in the leadership of church; find out different elements of dishonesty and nonaccountability found in some leaders of our church; find out the possible factors which bring about dishonesty and nonaccountability among leaders of Lutheran Church of Nigeria at their units; find out leadership of our church and determine the strategies that can help strengthen the integrity and accountability.

---

[10] Potter, "The Traits/Characteristics, Attitudes, and Effective Work Environments of Servant Leaders."

[11] Rubin, Dierdorff, and Brown, "Do Ethical Leaders Get Ahead?" 215–36.

APPENDIX FOUR

STRENGTHENING INTEGRITY AND ACCOUNTABILITY IN THE LEADERSHIP OF LUTHERAN CHURCH OF NIGERIA THROUGH PERFORMANCE MANAGEMENT[1]

By Christian Ekong, President/Archbishop, Lutheran Church of Nigeria

INTRODUCTION

The expression "performance management" is not found anywhere in the Bible. Yet it includes three distinct stages that, when correctly applied, spur Christians in the Church on to even greater accomplishments in their next task, simultaneously improving or strengthening their capacity and increasing their desire.

The stages are:

1. Goal setting and motivation
2. Encouragement
3. Rewards and consequences

Many of the following ideas are based upon Lorin Woolfe's *The Bible on Leadership*.[2] In a sense, the fall of Adam and Eve could be seen as a leadership failure. The Lord created Adam first and gave him the one commandment, "You shall not eat of the fruit of the tree in the middle of the garden." When the serpent appeared, Eve carried on conversation while Adam stood nearby. Adam, who had been given the responsibility to teach the command to Eve, did not step up and repeat the command to Eve and the serpent. Or consider Noah, who worked for 120 years to build an ark. There was no indication that a worldwide flood was coming. He trusted God's Word and

[1] Lecture Presentation at LCN 3rd Biennial Convention. This presentation has been changed for publication.

[2] Lorin Woolfe, *The Bible on Leadership—From Moses to Matthew, Management Lessons for Contemporary Leaders*, AMACOM, 2002.

endured much scorn and mocking from the world as he built his giant boat on dry land. He encouraged his family to continue on the task despite the challenges.

Even the best leader needs faithful, passionate followers to achieve maximum performance: Moses encouraged his people during forty years in the desert. David encouraged his son Solomon to realize the daunting scope of building the first temple.

Jesus called His disciples to leave behind their careers as fishermen to become fishers of men. Being a leader can take the patience of Job, David's courage, and Solomon's wisdom. Jesus led unlike any leader with compassion.

The Bible is not a manual on leadership, but we can see leadership examples in the Bible. We can recognize that leadership both in the Bible and in the secular world has a lot to do with First Article gifts. Church leaders can aspire to be the best leaders they possibly can be.

Before we proceed to discuss the three stages, kindly review our 38th Council Presentation on Integrity and Accountability in LCN leadership.

1. What integrity is
2. What accountability is
3. The theological focus of integrity and accountability in leadership of church

Motivation and Goal Setting

The first task for a leader in performance management is to set realistic, achievable goals. The leader helps motivate the people to follow through with these goals. In 1 Thess. 2:6–12, St. Paul was gentle toward the people. He worked to reduce their burdens; in fact, he took no salary from the Thessalonians. He acted as a father does toward his children and he encouraged them.

Inspiration

A leader inspires people to achieve a common set of goals and encourages people to work toward these goals. The leader inspires his followers to accomplish the organization's goals. For example, Moses inspired the people of Israel to cross the desert to the edge of the Promised Land. Nehemiah, in the face of great opposition, inspired God's people to rebuild the wall around Jerusalem. Jesus called His disciples by calling them to become fishers of men (Mark 1:17).

Encouragement

Moses knew how powerful encouragement is to achieving important goals. When the desert sands looked unending, the Israelites cried out with hunger, and when internal dissidents threatened to undermine the goal of possessing the "land of milk and honey," crying out to return to Egypt, Moses reminded the Israelites that the land truly existed, even if they had not seen it. Church leaders often forget that people look up to hear the truth of how they are doing. We acknowledge the difficulty of doing this gently and positively. Difficult tasks require ongoing encouragement. Barnabas, one of Jesus' disciples, was originally called Joseph, but he was given his new name, which means "son of encouragement." Encouragement is rooted in the Latin for "heart." Moses encouraged the tribes of Israel by blessing them.

Punishment and reproach discourages people, while blessing encourages people. This is built into our nature and is similar to the theological principle of Law and Gospel. God's Law kills the sinner, while the Gospel gives life and salvation.

Rewards

There is power in positive rewards, even words of appreciation. Positive rewards develop loyalty and commitment to future performance. A leader who rewards his people will achieve more than one who does not. As St. Paul says in 1 Cor. 3:8, "each will receive his wages according to his labor."

We can mirror Joshua's generosity toward his followers—the Reubenites, the Gadites, and the half-tribe of Manasseh—all of whom had helped him conquer the neighboring tribes: "You have kept all that Moses . . . commanded. . . . You have not forsaken your brothers these many days, down to this day, but have been careful to keep the charge of the LORD your God. . . . Go back to your tents with much wealth. . . . Divide the spoil of your enemies with your brothers" (Josh. 22:2–3, 8). There is power in positive rewards, even words of appreciation. Positive rewards develop loyalty and commitment to future performance.

Firm But Fair Practices

Combining structured, exacting behavior and performance with kindness and impartiality is a balance that is difficult to achieve. However, leaders who are able to do so receive a high level of loyalty from their "followership" and congregation. Phil Meyers, the account manager of Service Master Company, set a three-step process to follow in achieving excellent work:

1. Confront the negative behaviors.
2. Give the employee a chance to change.
3. Terminate if there is no improvement.[3]

Conclusion

Finally, we can see strengthening integrity and accountability in Christian leadership on the biblical principles of:

1. "Stop sinning, or something worse may happen to you" (John 5:14).
2. "Yet now I am happy because your sorrow led to repentance" (2 Cor. 7:8).
3. "I will discipline you, but only with justice" (Jer. 10:24).

As leaders, we should regularly communicate performance expectations before, during, and after our task.

The Lord is with you! Amen.

[3] Woolfe, *The Bible on Leadership*, 117.

BIBLIOGRAPHY

Akpami, John E. *Leadership with Results*. Kaduna, Nigeria: TW Press & Publishers, 2006.

———. *Vision: Equipping Church Workers for Effective Leadership*. Kaduna, Nigeria: TW Press & Publishers, 2002.

Albritton, M. David, Sharon L. Oswald, and Joseph S. Anderson. "Leadership Quality and Follower Affect: A Study of U. S. Presidential Candidates." *Journal of Leadership Studies* 1, no. 4 (2008): 6–22. https://onlinelibrary.wiley.com/doi/abs/10.1002/jls.20035.

Allix, Nicholas M. "Transformational Leadership: Democratic or Despotic?" *Educational Management & Administration* 28, no. 1 (January 1, 2000): 7–20. https://doi.org/10.1177/0263211X000281002.

Andvig, Jens Christian, Odd Helge Fjeldstad, Inge Amundsen, Tone Sissener, and Tina Søreide. *Research on Corruption: A Policy Oriented Survey*. Bergen, Norway: Chr. Michelsen Institute, 2000. http://www.cmi.no.

Annis, A. "The Future of Leadership in Learning Organizations." *Journal of Leadership Studies* 7, no. 3 (1987): 119.

Atado, J. C. *The Leader We Want*. Kano, Nigeria: Modern Printers, 2011.

Awamleh, Raed, and William L. Gardner. "Perceptions of Leader Charisma and Effectiveness: The Effects of Vision Content, Delivery, and Organizational Performance." *The Leadership Quarterly* 10, no. 3 (September 1, 1999): 345–73. http://www.sciencedirect.com/science/article/pii/S1048984399000223.

Badaracco, Joseph L., and Richard R. Ellsworth. *Leadership and the Quest for Integrity*. Boston: Harvard Business School Press, 1989.

Banisar, David. *Freedom of Information around the World 2006: A Global Survey of Access to Government Records Laws*. London: Privacy International, 2006.

Banks, Robert. *Reviewing Leadership: A Christian Evaluation of Current Approaches*. Grand Rapids: Baker Academic, 2004.

Barrett, David B., Todd M. Johnson, Christopher R. Guidry, and Peter F. Crossing. *World Christian Trends, AD 30–AD 2200: Interpreting the Annual Christian Megacensus*. Pasadena, Calif.: William Carey Library, 2001. http://hdl.library.upenn.edu/1017.12/366304.

———, George Thomas Kurian, and Todd M. Johnson. *World Christian Encyclopedia: A Comparative Survey of Churches and Religions in the Modern World*. Second edition. Oxford: Oxford University Press, 2001.

Bass, Bernard M. *Leadership and Performance beyond Expectations*. New York: Free Press, 1985.

———. *Transformational Leadership*. Second edition. Mahwah, N.J.: L. Erlbaum Associates, 2006.

Beach, Dale S. *Personnel: The Management of People at Work*. Fifth edition. New York: Macmillan, 1985.

Becker, Thomas E. "Integrity in Organizations: Beyond Honesty and Conscientiousness." *Academy of Management Review* 23, no. 1 (January 1, 1998): 154–61. https://journals.aom.org/doi/10.5465/amr.1998.192969.

Bennis, Warren G., and Joan Goldsmith. *Learning to Lead: A Workbook on Becoming a Leader*. Fourth edition, revised and updated. 1 online resource (xxiii, 240 pages): illustrations vols. New York: Basic Books, 2010. http://public.eblib.com/choice/publicfullrecord.aspx?p=515497.

Berger, Peter L. *The Desecularization of the World: Resurgent Religion and World Politics*. Washington DC: Ethics and Public Policy Center, 2008.

Boerner, Sabine, and Christian Freiherr von Streit. "Transformational Leadership and Group Climate-Empirical Results from Symphony Orchestras." *Journal of Leadership & Organizational Studies* 12, no. 2 (July 21, 2016): 31–41. https://journals.sagepub.com/doi/pdf/10.1177/107179190501200203.

Boje, David M., and Carl Rhodes. "The Virtual Leader Construct: The Mass Mediatization and Simulation of Transformational Leadership." *Leadership* (August 11, 2016). https://journals.sagepub.com/doi/pdf/10.1177/1742715005057232.

Brown, Michael E., Linda K. Treviño, and David A. Harrison. "Ethical Leadership: A Social Learning Perspective for Construct Development and Testing." *Organizational Behavior and Human Decision Processes* 97, no. 2 (July 1, 2005): 117–34. http://www.sciencedirect.com/science/article/pii/S0749597805000397.

Bruce, Steve. "Secularisation, Church and Popular Religion." *The Journal of Ecclesiastical History* 62, no. 3 (July 2011): 543–61.

Bruch, Heike, and Frank Walter. "Leadership in Context: Investigating Hierarchical Impacts on Transformational Leadership." *Leadership & Organization Development Journal* 28, no. 8 (November 6, 2007): 710–26. https://www.emeraldinsight.com/doi/abs/10.1108/01437730710835452.

Calder, Bobby J. "An Attribution Theory of Leadership." Pages 179–204 in *New Directions in Organizational Behavior*. Edited by Barry M. Staw and Gerald R. Salancik. Chicago: St. Clair Press, 1977.

Collver, Albert B. *Ezra and Nehemiah: The Lord Is Faithful*. God's Word for Today. St. Louis: Concordia, 2009.

Cooper, Michael. "The Transformational Leadership of the Apostle Paul: A Contextual and Biblical Leadership for Contemporary Ministry." *Christian Education Journal* (March 14, 2018). https://journals.sagepub.com/doi/pdf/10.1177/073989130500200103.

Cooper, Robert. "Peripheral Vision: Relationality." *Organization Studies* 26, no. 11 (2005): 1689–710.

Cordeiro, Wayne. *Doing Church as a Team: The Miracle of Teamwork and How It Transforms Churches*. Ventura, Calif.: Regal Books, 2005.

Covey, Stephen R. *Principle-Centered Leadership*. New York: Summit Books, 1991.

Currie, Graeme, Inger Boyett, and Olga Suhomlinova. "Transformational Leadership within Secondary Schools in England: A Panacea for Organizational Ills?" *Public Administration* 83, no. 2 (June 1, 2005): 265–96. https://onlinelibrary.wiley.com/doi/abs/10.1111/j.0033-3298.2005.00450.x.

———, and Andy Lockett. "A Critique of Transformational Leadership: Moral, Professional and Contingent Dimensions of Leadership within Public Services Organizations." *Human Relations* 60, no. 2 (2007): 341–70.

Driscoll, Cathy, and Margaret McKee. "Restorying a Culture of Ethical and Spiritual Values: A Role for Leader Storytelling." *Journal of Business Ethics* 73, no. 2 (June 1, 2007): 205–17. https://doi.org/10.1007/s10551-006-9191-5.

Druskat, Vanessa Urch. "Gender and Leadership Style: Transformational and Transactional Leadership in the Roman Catholic Church." *The Leadership Quarterly* 5, no. 2 (1994): 99–119.

Eighinger, L. *Condensed Version of the Study of Ethics*. The Interpreter's Friend, 1998. http://www.theinterpretersfriend.org/Terpsnet/6.html.

Eisenbeiss, Silke A., Daan van Knippenberg, and Sabine Boerner. "Transformational Leadership and Team Innovation: Integrating Team Climate Principles." *Journal of Applied Psychology* 93, no. 6 (2008): 1438–46. https://pdfs.semanticscholar.org/7ee2/b434a08c2e358e3e2500a3c197d6caf2dee3.pdf.

Emery, Charles R., and Katherine J. Barker. "The Effect of Transactional and Transformational Leadership Styles on the Organizational Commitment and Job Satisfaction of Customer Contact Personnel." *Journal of Organizational Culture, Communications and Conflict* 11, no. 1 (January 1, 2007): 77. https://www.questia.com/library/journal/1G1-166935405/the-effect-of-transactional-and-transformational-leadership.

Epitropaki, Olga, and Robin Martin. "Implicit Leadership Theories in Applied Settings: Factor Structure, Generalizability, and Stability over Time." *The Journal of Applied Psychology* 89, no. 2 (April 2004): 293–310.

———. "The Moderating Role of Individual Differences in the Relation between Transformational/Transactional Leadership Perceptions and Organizational Identification." *The Leadership Quarterly* 16, no. 4. Leadership, Self, and Identity (August 1, 2005): 569–89. http://www.sciencedirect.com/science/article/pii/S1048984305000639.

Fisher, J. R. "What Will It Take to Transform Your Organization in the 21st Century?" *Journal for Quality & Participation* 22, no. 6 (2009).

Foti, R. J., S. L. Fraser, and R. G. Lord. "Effects of Leadership Labels and Prototypes on Perceptions of Political Leaders." *Journal of Applied Psychology* 67, no. 3 (1982): 326–33.

———, and Carissa H. Luch. "The Influence of Individual Differences on the Perception and Categorization of Leaders." *The Leadership Quarterly* 3, no. 1 (March 1, 1992): 55–66. http://www.sciencedirect.com/science/article/pii/1048984392900062.

Freeman, R. Edward, and Lisa Stewart. *Developing Ethical Leadership*. Bridge Papers. Charlottesville, Va.: Business Roundtable Institute for Corporate Ethics, 2000.

Fry, Louis W. "Toward a Theory of Spiritual Leadership." *The Leadership Quarterly* 14, no. 6 (December 1, 2003): 693–727. http://www.sciencedirect.com/science/article/pii/S1048984303000547.

———, Steve Vitucci, and Marie Cedillo. "Spiritual Leadership and Army Transformation: Theory, Measurement, and Establishing a Baseline." *The Leadership Quarterly* 16, no. 5. Toward a Paradigm of Spiritual Leadership (October 1, 2005): 835–62. http://www.sciencedirect.com/science/article/pii/S1048984305000779.

Gerstner, Charlotte R., and David V. Day. "Cross-Cultural Comparison of Leadership Prototypes." *The Leadership Quarterly* 5, no. 2 (June 1, 1994): 121–34. http://www.sciencedirect.com/science/article/pii/1048984394900248.

Gibson, Kevin. "Excuses, Excuses: Moral Slippage in the Workplace." *Business Horizons* 43, no. 6 (November 1, 2000): 65–72. http://www.sciencedirect.com/science/article/pii/S0007681300800245.

Graen, George B., and Mary Uhl-Bien. "Relationship-Based Approach to Leadership: Development of Leader-Member Exchange (LMX) Theory of Leadership over 25 Years: Applying a Multi-Level Multi-Domain Perspective." *The Leadership Quarterly* 6, no. 2 (June 1, 1995): 219–47. http://www.sciencedirect.com/science/article/pii/1048984395900365.

Grothe, Jonathan F. *Reclaiming Patterns of Pastoral Ministry: Jesus and Paul*. Concordia Scholarship Today. St. Louis: Concordia, 1988.

Hartog, Deanne N. Den, Robert J. House, Paul J. Hanges, S. Antonio Ruiz-Quintanilla, and Peter W. Dorfman. "Culture Specific and Cross-Culturally Generalizable Implicit Leadership Theories: Are Attributes of Charismatic/Transformational Leadership Universally Endorsed?" *The Leadership Quarterly* 10, no. 2 (June 1, 1999): 219–56. http://www.sciencedirect.com/science/article/pii/S1048984399000181.

Heward-Mills, Dag. *The Art of Leadership*. Second edition. [Accra, Ghana]: Parchment House, 2006.

Hinkin, Timothy R., and Chester A. Schriesheim. "A Theoretical and Empirical Examination of the Transactional and Non-Leadership Dimensions of the Multifactor Leadership Questionnaire (MLQ)." *The Leadership Quarterly* 19, no. 5 (October 1, 2008): 501–13. http://www.sciencedirect.com/science/article/pii/S1048984308000933.

———. "An Examination of 'Nonleadership': From Laissez-Faire Leadership to Leader Reward Omission and Punishment Omission." *The Journal of Applied Psychology* 93, no. 6 (November 2008): 1234–48.

Hornby, Albert Sydney. *Oxford Advanced Learner's Dictionary of Current English*. Oxford: Oxford University Press, 2001.

House, Robert J. "Path-Goal Theory of Leadership: Lessons, Legacy, and a Reformulated Theory." *The Leadership Quarterly* 7, no. 3 (September 1, 1996): 323–52. http://www.sciencedirect.com/science/article/pii/S1048984396900247.

Hoy, Wayne K., and Cecil G. Miskel. *Educational Administration: Theory, Research, and Practice*. New York: Random House, 1982.

Hunt, J. G., Kimerly B. Boal, and Ritch L. Sorenson. "Top Management Leadership: Inside the Black Box." *The Leadership Quarterly* 1, no. 1 (March 1, 1990): 41–65. http://www.sciencedirect.com/science/article/pii/1048984390900149.

Hybels, Bill. *Courageous Leadership*. Grand Rapids: Zondervan, 2002.

Ibanga, U. A. *Statistics for Social Sciences*. Jos, Nigeria: Centre for Development Studies, University of Jos, 1992.

Jackall, Robert. *Moral Mazes: The World of Corporate Managers*. Oxford: Oxford University Press, 2010.

Kaye, Anders. "Resurrecting the Causal Theory of the Excuses." *Nebraska Law Review* 83, no. 4 (2005): 1117–77. http://digitalcommons.unl.edu/nlr/vol83/iss4/4.

Kearney, Eric, and Diether Gebert. "Managing Diversity and Enhancing Team Outcomes: The Promise of Transformational Leadership." *Journal of Applied Psychology* 94, no. 1 (2009): 77–89.

Kelley, Robert Earl. *The Power of Followership: How to Create Leaders People Want to Follow, and Followers Who Lead Themselves*. First edition. New York: Doubleday, 2002.

Knowles, Elizabeth. *The Oxford Dictionary of Quotations*. Fifth edition. Oxford: Oxford University Press, 1999.

Laub, James A. "Organizational Health." *Servant Leader Performance*, n.d. https://olagroup.com/Display.asp?Page=organizational_health.

Lourens, Jan Francois. "Change-Centred Leadership and Various Correlates." PhD dissertation, University of Pretoria, 2007. http://hdl.handle.net/2263/24931.

Luther, Martin. *Luther's Small Catechism with Explanation*. St. Louis: Concordia, 1986.

———. "Treatise on Christian Liberty." Translated by Henry Jacobs in *Works of Martin Luther*. Philadelphia: A. J. Holman, 1915.

McCaslin, Mark L. "The Landscape of Leadership Building Relationships." *Journal of Leadership Studies* (September 14, 2016). https://journals.sagepub.com/doi/pdf/10.1177/107179190100800202.

Munroe, Myles. *Becoming a Leader*. New Kensington, Penn.: Whitaker House, 2009.

Ngu, S. M. *Management Principles and Workers Motivation in Nigeria*. Zaria, Nigeria: Gaskiya Corporation Ltd., 2005.

Niebuhr, H. Richard. *The Social Sources of Denominationalism*. Hamden, Conn.: Shoe String Press, 1954.

Nwolise, Nwakibiye P. C. *Traditional Administration in Nigeria: Historical Perspective, Theory and Practice*. Port Harcourt, Nigeria: Paragraphics, 2009.

Okoronta, G. O. "The Impact of Leadership Styles in the Pentecostal Churches on the Growth of the Gospel in Kaduna State." Ahmadu Bello University, 2015.

Onuogu, R. C. *Creative Leadership*. Lagos, Nigeria: Touchlife, 2008.

Organisation for Economic Co-operation and Development. *Integrity in Public Procurement: Good Practice from A to Z*. Paris: OECD, 2007.

Peterson, Eugene H. *Working the Angles: The Shape of Pastoral Integrity*. New edition. Grand Rapids: Eerdmans, 1993.

Potter, Dorothy O. "The Traits/Characteristics, Attitudes, and Effective Work Environments of Servant Leaders: A Delphi Study." PhD dissertation, Capella University, 2009. http://search.proquest.com/docview/305160274/abstract/344013EF0894095PQ/1.

Purvanova, Radostina K., Joyce E. Bono, and Jessica Dzieweczynski. "Transformational Leadership, Job Characteristics, and Organizational Citizenship Performance." *Human Performance* 19, no. 1 (January 2006): 1–22.

Rieke, Mark L., and Stephen J. Guastello. "Unresolved Issues in Honesty and Integrity Testing." *American Psychologist* 50, no. 6 (June 1995): 458.

Rubin, Robert S., Erich C. Dierdorff, and Michael E. Brown. "Do Ethical Leaders Get Ahead? Exploring Ethical Leadership and Promotability." *Business Ethics Quarterly* 20, no. 2 (2010): 215–36. https://www.jstor.org/stable/25702394.

Sampson, Anthony. *Mandela: The Authorized Biography*. New York: Vintage Books, 2011.

Shawchuck, Norman, and Roger Heuser. *Leading the Congregation: Caring for Yourself While Serving Others*. Nashville: Abingdon Press, 1993.

Simons, Tony. "Behavioral Integrity as a Critical Ingredient for Transformational Leadership." *Journal of Organizational Change Management* 12, no. 2 (1999): 89–104. https://doi.org/10.1108/09534819910263640.

Strudler, Alan, and Danielle E. Warren. "Authority, Heuristics, and the Structure of Excuses." Pages 155–78 in *Social Influences on Ethical Behavior in Organizations*. Edited by John M. Darley, David M. Messick, and Tom R. Taylor. Mahwah, N.J.: L. Erlbaum, 2001.

Van Gelder, Craig., ed. *The Missional Church and Leadership Formation: Helping Congregations Develop Leadership Capacity*. Missional Church Series. Grand Rapids: Eerdmans, 2009.

Weber, Max. *The Protestant Ethic and the Spirit of Capitalism*. New York: Scribner, 1930. http://archive.org/details/protestantethics00webe.

Witte, John. "The Freedom of a Christian: Martin Luther's Reformation of Law and Liberty." *Evangelische Theologie* 74, no. 2 (2014): 127–35.

Wong, Paul T. P., and Don Page. "Servant Leadership: An Opponent-Process Model and the Revised Servant Leadership Profile." In *Proceedings of the Servant Leadership Research Roundtable*. University Park, Penn.: Servant Leadership Research Roundtable, 2003. http://citeseerx.ist.psu.edu/viewdoc/download?doi=10.1.1.714.6333&rep=rep1&type=pdf.

Wood, M. "Adventures of Difference in Leadership Studies." In *Paper Presented at EGOS 2006*. Bergen, Norway: EGOS, 2006.

Woolfe, Lorin. *The Bible on Leadership: From Moses to Matthew—Management Lessons for Contemporary Leaders*. New York: American Management Association, 2002.

Yuchtman, Ephraim, and Stanley E. Seashore. "A System Resource Approach to Organizational Effectiveness." *American Sociological Review* 32, no. 6 (1967): 891–903.

Zaccaro, Stephen J., and Zachary N. J. Horn. "Leadership Theory and Practice: Fostering an Effective Symbiosis." *Leadership Quarterly* 14, no. 6 (December 2003): 769.

PGIL2024USA